PROPERTY: TAKINGS

by

DAVID A. DANA
Professor of Law, Northwestern University

and

THOMAS W. MERRILL
John Paul Stevens Professor of Law, Northwestern
University

D0841105

TURNING POINT SERIES®

New York, New York
FOUNDATION PRESS
2002

Turning Point Series is a registered trademark
used herein under license.

COPYRIGHT © 2002 By FOUNDATION PRESS

> 395 Hudson Street
> New York, NY 10014
> Phone Toll Free 1–877–888–1330
> Fax (212) 367–6799
> fdpress.com

All rights reserved
Printed in the United States of America

ISBN 1–58778–078–X

TEXT IS PRINTED ON 10% POST
CONSUMER RECYCLED PAPER

TURNING POINT SERIES

CIVIL PROCEDURE

Civil Procedure: Class Actions by Linda S. Mullenix, University of Texas (Available 2003)

Civil Procedure: Economics of Civil Procedure by Robert G. Bone, Boston University (Available October 2002)

Civil Procedure: Preclusion in Civil Actions by David L. Shapiro, Harvard University (2001)

Civil Procedure: Jury Process by Nancy S. Marder, Illinois Institute of Technology (Available December 2002)

Civil Procedure: Territorial Jurisdiction and Venue by Kevin M. Clermont, Cornell (1999)

CONSTITUTIONAL LAW

Constitutional Law: Equal Protection by Louis M. Seidman, Georgetown University (Available December 2002)

Constitutional Law: Religion Clause by Daniel O. Conkle, Indiana University, Bloomington (Available 2003)

CRIMINAL LAW

Criminal Law: Model Penal Code by Markus D. Dubber, State University of New York, Buffalo (2002)

Criminal Law: Habeas Corpus by Larry W. Yackle, Boston University (Available 2003)

INTERNATIONAL LAW

International Law: United States Foreign Relations Law by Phillip R. Trimble, UCLA (2002)

LEGISLATION

Legislation: Statutory Interpretation: Twenty Questions by Kent R. Greenawalt, Columbia University (1999)

PROPERTY

Property: Takings by David Dana, Northwestern University and Thomas Merrill, Northwestern University (2002)

CORPORATE/SECURITIES

Securities Law: Insider Trading by Stephen Bainbridge, UCLA (1999)

TORTS

Torts: Proximate Cause by Joseph A. Page, Georgetown University (Available December 2002)

For my parents Alfred and Estelle, and Julie, Emily, and Claire.

D.D.

For my father, W.M.M.

T.W.M.

*

Acknowledgements

The authors would like to thank Steve Calabresi, Joe Miller, Adam Mossoff, and Henry Smith for reading and commenting on portions of an earlier draft. Cathy Gerlach and David Marquez provided valuable research assistance.

*

About the Authors

David Dana is Professor of Law at Northwestern University School of Law, and specializes in property, land use and environmental law.

Thomas Merrill is John Paul Stevens Professor of Law at Northwestern University, and specializes in administrative law, constitutional law, and property.

*

TABLE OF CONTENTS

*

PROPERTY: TAKINGS

*

CHAPTER I

INTRODUCTION

"[N]or shall private property be taken for public use without just compensation."

—U.S. CONST., amend. V.

Property owners have, at different times in our history, secured protection for their interests under different provisions of the Constitution. In the first half of the Nineteenth Century, the Contract Clause of Article I, section 10 was the most important source of constitutional constraint. Later in that century and up through early years of the New Deal, the doctrine of substantive due process associated with *Lochner v. New York*[1] came to the fore. Today, the Takings Clause, the text of which is quoted above, has become the most important source of constitutional protection available to property owners.

As part of the original Bill of Rights, the Takings Clause directly constrains the federal government.[2] The protection afforded by the Clause has also been applied to the States through the Due Process

1. 198 U.S. 45 (1905).

2. *See* Barron v. Baltimore, 32 U.S. (7 Pet.) 243, 250–51 (1833).

1

Clause of the Fourteenth Amendment.[3] The Supreme Court generally has employed the same standards in assessing takings claims without regard to whether the action is brought against the federal government under the Fifth Amendment or against a State under the Fourteenth. In addition, all state constitutions (except North Carolina's) include takings clauses,[4] with the result that state governments are subject to parallel federal and state constitutional restrictions when they engage in takings of property. With some variations, these state takings clauses have been interpreted by state courts in the same manner as the federal Takings Clause.

One cannot make sense of judicial decisions interpreting the Takings Clause without understanding that the Clause functions primarily as a limitation on the power of eminent domain. During the early decades of our constitutional history, when the Contract Clause and substantive due process were the most important sources of protection for property rights, the Takings Clause operated almost exclusively as a limitation on the power of eminent domain. This remains its core function today. Moreover, although the modern Supreme Court has extended the Clause beyond the eminent domain context, the key justification for doing so has been the need to police attempts by the government to evade

3. *See* Chicago, Burlington & Quincy R.R. Co. v. City of Chicago, 166 U.S. 226, 238–39 (1897).

4. 1 Philip Nichols, Nichols' The Law of Eminent Domain § 1.3, at 1–95 (Julius Sackman ed., 3d ed. 2001).

the constitutional limitation that the Clause places on eminent domain.

Eminent domain is an inherent attribute of sovereignty, recognized by all fifty States and the federal government.[5] Although the power is originally vested in the legislature, it is often delegated to other entities, such as municipalities, government agencies, public utility companies, and common carriers. An entity to which the power of eminent domain has been properly delegated may acquire private property without the consent of the owner, usually through a judicial proceeding called a condemnation action. This power to engage in forced exchanges of property is used for a variety of purposes. These include the acquisition of land or interests in land for the construction of highways, utility lines, and government buildings; the acquisition of land or interests in land for urban renewal and natural resource conservation projects; and the acquisition of technology covered by patents and works of authorship covered by copyrights through the government procurement process.[6]

The Takings Clause does not shield property rights from being taken for public use by eminent

5. *See* Kohl v. United States, 91 U.S. 367, 371–75 (1875) (holding that eminent domain is an inherent attribute of sovereignty, and that the federal government has such power even if it is not expressly conferred by the Constitution).

6. A federal statute, 28 U.S.C. § 1498, authorizes the federal government to use patented technology and copyrighted works without the owner's consent but upon payment of just compensation. The Supreme Court has characterized this as an exercise of the power of eminent domain. *See* Crozier v. Fried. Krupp Aktiengesellschaft, 224 U.S. 290, 307 (1912).

domain. Rather, it requires that when the government engages in such forced exchanges, it must provide "just compensation" to the owner. The Clause thus transforms the power of eminent domain into a different sort of power from other attributes of government sovereignty, such as the power to tax, the power to wage war, or the police power (the power to regulate to protect public health and safety). These other governmental powers are not constrained by any constitutional requirement that the government compensate citizens for losses they incur when the power is exercised.[7] The Takings Clause is unique in requiring compensation in conjunction with the exercise of a certain type of governmental power—eminent domain—and it has been held to abrogate any claim of sovereign immunity that might otherwise stand as a barrier to the payment of such compensation.[8]

Although originally confined to exercises of eminent domain, the Supreme Court eventually extended the Takings Clause beyond that context. The watershed decision in this regard was *Pennsylvania Coal Co. v. Mahon*,[9] where the Court recognized that sometimes a police power regulation has an impact functionally equivalent to an exercise of eminent domain. In these circumstances, the Court

7. *See* Mugler v. Kansas, 123 U.S. 623, 668–69 (1887) (holding that exercise of the police power to prevent individuals from using their property to inflict injury on the community does not require payment of compensation).

8. First English Evangelical Lutheran Church of Glendale v. Los Angeles County, 482 U.S. 304, 316 n. 9 (1987).

9. 260 U.S. 393 (1922).

held, the government may persist in regulating only if it pays just compensation. In other words, the government cannot evade the limits the Takings Clause imposes on the power of eminent domain by seeking to accomplish the same result through an exercise of the police power. *Mahon* gave rise to what has been called the "inverse condemnation" theory, or, as it is called more commonly today, the "regulatory takings" doctrine: If an exercise of the police power "goes too far" in interfering with property rights, it will be invalidated unless the government pays just compensation.[10]

As applied to conventional exercises of eminent domain, the Takings Clause presents basically three constitutional questions. The first is whether the interest of the claimant that has been taken is "private property." Only private property is entitled to just compensation when taken. The second is whether the condemnation is for a "public use." The Court has construed the Takings Clause to mean that takings for purely private uses are beyond the power of the government, although it has given the legislature the benefit of the doubt as to what constitutes a legitimate public use.[11] The third is whether the payment offered by the government constitutes the "just compensation" required by the Constitution. Courts independently scrutinize condemnation awards to insure that they are "just."

10. *Id.* at 415.

11. *See* Hawaii Hous. Auth. v. Midkiff, 467 U.S. 229, 240–41 (1984) (rejecting claim that condemnation of landlords' reversionary interests under long-term leases as part of a state land reform program was not a legitimate public use).

The regulatory takings doctrine recognized in *Mahon* can present each of the three foregoing questions. In addition, however, regulatory takings cases present a fourth issue: whether the challenged regulation is a "taking," as opposed to a legitimate exercise of the police power for which there is no obligation to pay just compensation. This issue does not arise when the government engages in formal exercises of eminent domain, because a condemnation proceeding results in a judicial judgment that transfers title from the prior owner to the condemning authority, and there is no doubt that this is a "taking." Determining what constitutes a "taking" when the government adopts a regulation that stops short of acquiring title to the property has proven to be an especially vexing issue, and has produced a number of sharply divided opinions of the Supreme Court.

The controversy over the regulatory takings doctrine has also stimulated a large and growing scholarly literature about the underlying purpose of the Takings Clause. Some of this literature seeks to uncover the original understanding of the Takings Clause. Chapter II reviews what little is known about why the Framers included the Takings Clause in the Bill of Rights, and what inferences can be drawn from what we do know. Other scholars have sought to develop a general theory of why the government should compensate individuals who suffer disproportionate losses because of government actions, and to use this theory as a guide to proper interpretation of the Takings Clause. Chapter III summarizes three prominent strands of takings theory that have been advanced in recent years, which we label "equal treatment," "fiscal illusion," and "process failure" theories.

The next five chapters take a closer look at more discrete legal issues presented by the language of the Clause. Chapter IV addresses what it means to take "private property"; Chapters V and VI examine how courts resolve controversies over what constitutes a "taking"; Chapter VII explores questions about what constitutes "just compensation"; and Chapter VIII looks at the meaning of the "public use" language.

The final three chapters address additional issues of doctrinal importance. Chapter IX considers cases that have applied the unconstitutional conditions doctrine to exactions of private property rights in the context of land use planning. Chapter X is devoted to emerging issues about takings of intangible rights, including intellectual property rights and regulatory contracts. Chapter XI offers an overview of some of the unique issues that arise in litigating takings claims.

CHAPTER II

THE ORIGINAL UNDERSTANDING
OF THE TAKINGS CLAUSE

There is disagreement about how much weight should be given to evidence of original understanding in interpreting the Constitution. As a rule, conservatives tend to advocate interpreting the Constitution in accordance with the public meaning of the document at the time of the framing; liberals are more likely to endorse an evolutionary interpretation based on a conception of the Constitution's underlying purposes. This debate carries over into judicial decisions and commentary about the Takings Clause. Here, however, we find an inversion of usual positions: When disputes about the scope and meaning of the Takings Clause arise, conservatives frequently can be found arguing for what amounts to a living Constitution, whereas liberals not uncommonly sound like originalists.[12] In this context

12. Thus, in Lucas v. South Carolina Coastal Council, 505 U.S. 1003 (1992), the Rehnquist Court's most important takings decision, Justice Scalia, writing for a majority of five Justices, dismissed as "entirely irrelevant" evidence that the Court's interpretation of the Takings Clause was inconsistent with "early American experience" and the views of "early constitutional theorists." *Id.* at 1028 n.15. Justice Blackmun, writing in dissent for four Justices, chastised the majority for adopting an interpretation at odds with the understandings reflected in early American practices and beliefs. *Id.* at 1055–60.

at least, commitments to constitutional method seem to matter less than do perceptions about the importance of protecting property rights from government interference. Conservatives tend to worry more about protecting property rights; liberals are more apt to be concerned about giving the government adequate room to regulate. These fundamental value commitments, not abstract commitments to principles of constitutional interpretation, drive our understanding of the Takings Clause.

There is, in fact, little direct evidence about the Framers' reasons for adopting the Takings Clause. We begin by summarizing the few known facts about the drafting history of the Clause, and some plausible inferences that can be drawn from that history. We then review the practices with respect to takings of property in England and the colonies prior to the adoption of the Bill of Rights. We conclude by considering what commentators familiar to the Framers had to say about the purposes of the power of eminent domain and the reasons for providing compensation when property is taken by the government.

A. The Drafting History

After the Constitution was approved at the Philadelphia Convention on September 17, 1787, it was submitted to the States to consider in special ratifying conventions. Most of these conventions recommended that a bill of rights be added to the Constitution. The States collectively proposed over 80 different amendments that might be incorporated into a bill of rights. Significantly, the Takings Clause or its equivalent was not among them.[13]

James Madison, who played a critical role at Philadelphia and co-authored the *Federalist Papers* arguing the case for ratification, was elected to the first Congress as a member of the House of Representatives from Virginia. He took it upon himself to distill the various state proposals into a draft bill of rights. When Madison unveiled his list of proposed amendments to the House in a speech on June 8, 1789, it included a new provision, not proposed by any State, that no person "be obliged to relinquish his property, where it may be necessary for public use, without a just compensation."[14]

Madison's amendments were referred to a select committee, consisting of one representative from each State. When the committee reported back to the House, the draft takings clause had been changed to its present form: "nor shall private property be taken for public use without just compensation."[15] Given this change, there must have been some discussion within the committee about Madison's proposal. However, the committee's deliberations were not recorded.[16]

13. *See* EDWARD DUMBAULD, THE BILL OF RIGHTS AND WHAT IT MEANS TODAY 162 (2d ed. 1979) (table).

14. 1 ANNALS OF CONG. 452 (Joseph Gales ed., 1789); *see also* DUMBAULD, *supra* note 13, at 207.

15. DUMBAULD, *supra* note 13, at 211.

16. The select committee's language was both broader and narrower than Madison's original language in certain respects.

Although the full House debated and revised a number of the proposed amendments that emerged from the select committee, the Takings Clause was approved without change or discussion.[17] The Senate, which at that time did not keep a journal of its proceedings, also made no change in the relevant language. President Washington transmitted the proposed amendments to the States on October 2, 1789. Within two years, every State had agreed to ratify what became the Fifth Amendment, including the Takings Clause. Because memorials of what occurred in the state ratifying conventions are virtually nonexistent,[18] we again do not know what (if anything) was said about the Takings Clause during the ratification debates.

The closest thing that exists to a contemporaneous statement about the purposes of the Takings Clause is a comment by St. George Tucker in his edition of William Blackstone's *Commentaries*, which was published in 1803, but probably written

It was broader, in that Madison's original language spoke of "relinquishing" property to the government—implying a complete transfer of possession—rather than government "takings," which might occur without a transfer of possession. Madison also spoke of relinquishments that are "necessary" for public use, and the concept of necessity dropped out of the select committee's version. On the other hand, the select committee used the phrase "private property" rather than "property," arguably narrowing the Madisonian language. It is impossible to know what to make of these changes without further evidence as to whether the select committee intended any substantive change in Madison's original proposal.

17. ANNALS, *supra* note 14, at 781.

18. DANIEL A. FARBER & SUZANNA SHERRY, A HISTORY OF THE AMERICAN CONSTITUTION 243 (1990).

before 1795.[19] Tucker was Professor of Law at William & Mary, and his commentaries on Blackstone incorporated the first published legal analysis of the Bill of Rights. With respect to the Takings Clause, Tucker offered the following observation:

That part of the [Fifth Amendment] which declares that private property shall not be taken for public use, without just compensation, was probably intended to restrain the arbitrary and oppressive mode of obtaining supplies for the army, and other public uses, by impressment, as was too frequently practised during the revolutionary war, without any compensation whatever.[20]

19. 1 St. George Tucker, Blackstone's Commentaries: With Notes of Reference to the Constitution and Laws, of the Federal Government of the United States, and of the Commonwealth of Virginia (orig. ed. 1803, reprinted 1996). The editors of the 1996 reprint note that Tucker sought a publisher for his manuscript as early as 1795, indicating that it was completed before then. *Id.* at xii.

20. *Id.* at 305–06. *See also* Akhil Ahmar, The Bill of Rights 80 (1998) (citing a 1778 tract by John Jay "condemning 'the Practice of impressing Horses, Teems [sic], and Carriages by the military, without the Intervention of a civil Magistrate, and without any Authority from the Law of the Land.' "). Madison alluded to the Takings Clause in a 1792 essay, *see* James Madison, *Property*, Phila. Nat'l Gazette, Mar. 27, 1792, *reprinted in* Mind of the Founder: Sources on the Political Thought of James Madison 186–88 (Marvin Myers ed., 1981), but did not offer any opinion about the meaning of the Clause, other than to suggest that it prohibits taking property "directly" for public use "without indemnification to the owner." *Id.* at 188. This perhaps implies that Madison thought that "indirect" violations of property rights would not be covered, so that, for example, reducing the tariff on a particular category of goods with the result that a domestic manufacturing firm went out of business would not be covered by the Takings Clause. But it has always been assumed

As drafting history goes, this is pretty thin. Nevertheless, the history allows us to draw a few inferences about the Takings Clause.

First, we can safely infer that there was no public agitation for takings protection during the period from 1787–88 when the Constitution was being ratified. The States during this time were busy compiling lists of rights to be incorporated into a new federal bill of rights. Yet not a single State recommended a takings clause. It is possible that no one thought the federal government would have any occasion to take property. But, given the Constitution's grants of power to Congress to do things such as "establish Post Offices and post Roads,"[21] and given the recent experience with impressments by the army during the revolutionary war, mentioned by Tucker, it would not have taken much foresight to envision that the new federal government might engage in takings of property.

Second, we can reliably conclude that the Clause was the brainchild of James Madison. The Clause made no appearance in the history of the Bill of Rights until Madison slipped it into a list that purported to be a distillation of the rights proposed by the state conventions. This is not to say that Madison had no antecedents to draw upon. Two existing state constitutions and the Northwest Ordinance contained similar provisions, and Blackstone's *Commentaries* (available in an American

that the Clause does not extend to these kinds of indirect injuries to property values.

21. U.S. Const. art. I, § 8.

edition since 1771) included a favorable reference to the need to provide full indemnification for takings of property.[22] But the idea of including such a right in the new federal Constitution was pretty clearly Madison's alone.

Third, we can infer that once Madison proposed that a takings clause be included in the Bill of Rights, the idea encountered no significant opposition. Indeed, other than the unexplained revision that occurred in the House select committee, Madison's proposal elicited no recorded response whatever from any quarter. It is probably safe to conclude that "both Federalists and Anti–Federalists opposed uncompensated takings and agreed on the importance of protecting property rights against government intrusion."[23]

We can perhaps draw a more significant and higher-order conclusion from these inferences: *The Takings Clause most likely was perceived as effecting no change in the legal status quo with respect to*

22. *See* William Michael Treanor, Note, *The Origins and Original Significance of the Just Compensation Clause of the Fifth Amendment*, 94 YALE L.J. 694, 701–08 (1985) (discussing the background of the Vermont, Massachusetts, and Northwest Ordinance Territories takings clauses); 1 WILLIAM BLACKSTONE, COMMENTARIES ON THE LAWS OF ENGLAND *135 (1768). Blackstone's COMMENTARIES were published in England between 1765 and 1769; the first American printing by Robert Bell of Philadelphia occurred in 1771. Madison was clearly conversant with the COMMENTARIES, and quoted Blackstone's definition of property in an essay written shortly after ratification of the Bill of Rights. *See* MIND OF THE FOUNDER, *supra* note 20, at 186.

23. James W. Ely, Jr., *"That Due Satisfaction May be Made:" The Fifth Amendment and the Origins of the Compensation Principle*, 36 AM. J. LEGAL HIST. 1, 18 (1992).

government takings of property. If existing practices with respect to government takings of property had contained features that were troubling to the founding generation, most likely one or more of the States would have proposed a constitutional amendment on the subject. They did not. Similarly, if the message reflected in the Clause—that private property taken for public use requires the payment of just compensation—had been perceived as effecting a change in existing practice, this would have elicited some resistance. Instead, the provision sailed through the amendment process without comment.

Even Madison's pivotal role is consistent with the inference that the Framers were simply constitutionalizing the legal status quo. Madison, as Jennifer Nedelsky has recounted, worried that some day the great mass of Americans would have no property and would seek to expropriate the holdings of the few.[24] Someone harboring this vision might have been unconcerned with existing practices regarding the taking of property, but nevertheless might have wanted to include explicit protection against uncompensated takings as insurance against a troubled future when those practices might come under pressure.

In short, the most logical explanation for the silence that preceded Madison's proposal, and the indifferent acquiescence that followed it, is that the Takings Clause simply codified the established prac-

24. JENNIFER NEDELSKY, PRIVATE PROPERTY AND THE LIMITS OF AMERICAN CONSTITUTIONALISM 27–28, 204–05 (1990).

tice of providing compensation when property was condemned or appropriated for public uses.[25]

B. English and Colonial Practices

If the Takings Clause was regarded by the founding generation as an affirmation of the status quo, then perhaps the best guide to the original understanding is the practices with respect to government takings of property in effect at the time of the adoption of the Constitution. A number of studies have been undertaken in recent years in an effort to document those practices. The picture that emerges is fairly consistent: The general practice, both in England and in the colonies at the time of the Revolution, was to provide compensation when title or possession of property was transferred to the government by force of law.[26] More specifically

25. One might argue that the public was indifferent to the Takings Clause because it applied only to the federal government, and thus left existing state practices unaffected. *See* Andrew S. Gold, *Regulatory Takings and Original Intent: The Direct, Physical Takings Thesis "Goes Too Far,"* 49 Am. U. L. Rev. 181, 223–28 (1999). But if there were an expectation that the Takings Clause would require the federal government to follow different practices with respect to takings than the practices then being followed in the States, one would expect some evidence of interest in this proposition.

26. For a review of English practices, *see* William B. Stoebuck, *A General Theory of Eminent Domain,* 47 Wash. L. Rev. 553, 575–79 (1972). For colonial practices, *see* John F. Hart, *Colonial Land Use Law and its Significance for Modern Takings Doctrine,* 109 Harv. L. Rev. 1252 (1996).

> [W]hen substantial parcels of land were taken for public facilities—courthouses, prisons, churches, fortifications—statutes normally specified that the landowner would receive compensation equivalent in value to the land taken. Compensation was also generally provided when government took temporary possession of private property, as in the compulsory lodging of troops.[27]

Payment of compensation was the practice not only when the government appropriated formal title to property, but also when "land was taken, used by the government, or damaged pursuant to government authorization."[28]

Compensation was not always given in circumstances where it would be today, most notably in the case of undeveloped land taken for the construction of public roads.[29] Even here, however, compensation was the rule, especially with respect to urban land, and increasingly so over time with respect to rural land.[30] Moreover, the fact that some of the colonies did not always compensate for roads is readily explained by the fact that in colonial America, rural landowners would count themselves lucky to have a road intersecting their property. Improved access to the outside world increased the value of

27. Hart, *supra* note 26, at 1283.

28. *Id.* at 1284.

29. *See* MORTON J. HORWITZ, THE TRANSFORMATION OF AMERICAN LAW 1780–1860, at 63–66 (1977); William Michael Treanor, *The Original Understanding of the Takings Clause and the Political Process*, 95 COLUM. L. REV. 782, 787 (1995).

30. Ely, *supra* note 23, at 7–12; Stoebuck, *supra* note 26, at 579–83.

the remaining land, usually by more than value of the land lost for the road.[31] Thus, this particular practice does not suggest any understanding that governments should be allowed to take property for public use without making full indemnification.

On the other hand, it is also true that both English and colonial governments engaged in some vigorous regulation of the use of land, and no one suggested these sorts of regulations gave rise to an obligation to pay compensation.[32] Some of these regulations were classic nuisance control measures, designed to prohibit invasions of private property by gases, odors or other noxious elements emanating from other property. Others were precursors of modern zoning regulations, such as segregating particular uses of property in particular areas of towns, or restricting the construction of unsightly buildings, the planting of certain types of vegetation, or excessive numbers of persons in dwellings. Still others imposed obligations on owners to engage in affirmative acts, including "use it or lose it" regulations requiring owners to develop their property within a certain time or risk forfeiture, and regulations requiring owners to drain swamps.[33] There was no judicial precedent or established practice, either at the time of the founding or for several generations afterwards, suggesting a duty to com-

31. *See* Stoebuck, *supra* note 26, at 582–83.

32. *See* FRED BOSSELMAN ET AL., THE TAKING ISSUE 53–81 (1973) (reviewing English land use regulation before the Revolution); Hart, *supra* note 26 (reviewing colonial land use regulation).

33. *See generally* Hart, *supra* note 26, at 1259–81.

pensate owners when any of these types of regulations resulted in a decline in property values, as they surely did on some occasions.

The conclusions we can draw from a review of existing practices at the time of the founding are mostly negative. On the one hand, although it is often asserted that the Framers thought compensation should be paid only for "physical appropriations" of property,[34] this overstates the record. To be sure, the evidence clearly suggests that physical appropriation was the paradigm case in which compensation was regarded as appropriate. But there is no affirmative evidence suggesting that the Framers regarded the Takings Clause as being limited to physical appropriations.[35] At the same time, the record of colonial practice is also inconsistent with any claim that the Framers understood the police power to be limited to regulation of common-law nuisances.[36] For example, use-it-or-lose-it regulations were designed to spur economic development, not to control nuisances.

C. The Views of Commentators Familiar to the Framers

Although we can glean certain insights from considering pre-ratification takings practices, this tells

34. *See, e.g.,* Treanor, *supra* note 22, at 711.

35. *See* Gold, *supra* note 25, at 182.

36. *Cf. Lucas,* 505 U.S. at 1027–32 (ruling in the context of regulations that deprive an owner of all economic value of property that the nuisance exception is limited to regulations that track the common law of nuisance).

us little about the Framers' understanding of the purposes of the Takings Clause. The founding generation was evidently comfortable with the notion that the government could condemn property rights in certain circumstances, and believed that compensation should ordinarily be paid when this happened. But there are no significant statements from participants in the formulation of the Bill of Rights, or from contemporary interpretations of the Clause, that offer any insight into why these propositions were taken for granted. The best we can do in imagining what the Framers might have thought about the purposes of the Takings Clause is to consult the writings of contemporary commentators who may have been familiar to at least some of them.

English writers, including Blackstone, had little to say about why the government should have the power to engage in forced exchanges of property. The natural law writers of continental Europe, beginning with Hugo Grotius in the Seventeenth Century, were divided on the subject. Some took the position that eminent domain was needed to deal with cases of urgent necessity, such as putting up fortifications to stop an enemy or building a detour around an obstructed road.[37] Others thought that it

37. Samuel Pufendorf was the most prominent exponent of the "urgent necessity" explanation. *See* SAMUEL PUFENDORF, DE OFFICIO HOMINIS ET CIVIS JUXTA LEGEM NATURALEM LIBRI DUO 136 (Frank Gardner Moore trans., Oxford Univ. Press 1927) (1682); *see also* SAMUEL PUFENDORF, DE JURE NATURAE ET GENTIUM LIBRI

could be used to promote public utility, as in constructing public works, markets, and perhaps even churches and universities.[38]

As to why compensation should be paid when property is taken, the natural law writers were of one view: Compensation is necessary in order to preserve horizontal equity among property owners within the society. William Stoebuck, in his reconstruction of the natural law thinkers' views on eminent domain, argues that the underlying notion was the "just share"—that all similarly situated persons should make the same contribution to support the cost of government.[39] Takings of property impose a higher burden on some property owners than others, with the result that the just share could be restored only by making an offsetting payment of compensation. As Pufendorf put it:

> Natural equity is observed, if, when some contribution must be made to preserve a common thing

OCTO 1285 (C.H. Oldfather & W.A. Oldfather trans., Clarendon Press 1934) (1672). The fortification and highway detour examples are found in CORNELIUS VAN BYNKERSHOEK, QUAESTIONUM JURIS PUBLICI LIBRI DUO 218–221 (Frank Tenny trans., Clarendon Press 1930) (1737).

38. Grotius, who was apparently the first to coin the term "eminent domain," favored the broader public advantage view. HUGO GROTIUS, DE JURE BELLI AC PACIS LIBRI TRES 807 (Francis W. Kelsey trans., Carnegie Institution of Wash. 1925) (1646). The most extensive discussion of eminent domain among the continental writers, which documents the divisions among the authorities, is found in VAN BYNKERSHOEK, *supra* note 37. He mentions examples of the power being used to construct churches and universities.

39. Stoebuck, *supra* note 26, at 584.

by such as participate in its benefits, each of them contributes only his own share, and no one bears a greater burden than another. . . . [T]he supreme sovereignty will be able to seize that thing for the necessities of the state, on condition, however, that whatever exceeds the just share of its owners must be refunded them by other citizens.[40]

The same notion is found in Vattel's influential treatise, *The Law of Nations*.[41] Vattel drew the instructive parallel to the maritime rule of jettison, whereby all persons shipping cargo on a vessel agree to contribute proportionately to offset the loss of anyone whose goods are thrown overboard in a storm. Both the maritime rule and compensation for takings illustrate the principle that "the burdens of the State should be borne equally by all, or in just proportion."[42] This theme clearly anticipates modern "equal treatment" theories of compensation, which we discuss in the next chapter.

While the natural law thinkers justified compensation in terms of maintaining horizontal equity among different subjects of the sovereign, Blackstone's *Commentaries* introduced a different idea— that compensation is justified because it maintains vertical equity between subject and sovereign. This is what Blackstone says:

40. Pufendorf, De Jure Naturae Et Gentium Libri Octo *supra* note 37, at 1285.

41. 3 E. de Vattel, The Law of Nations or the Principles of Natural Law 96 (Charles G. Fenwick trans., Carnegie Institute of Wash. 1916) (1758).

42. *Id.*

[T]he public good is in nothing more essentially interested, than in the protection of every individual's private rights, as modeled by the municipal law. In this, and similar cases the legislature alone can, and indeed frequently does, interpose, and compel the individual to acquiesce. But how does it interpose and compel? Not by absolutely stripping the subject of his property in an arbitrary manner; but by giving him a full indemnification and equivalent for the injury thereby sustained. *The public is now considered as an individual, treating with an individual for an exchange.* All the legislature does is to oblige the owner to alienate his possessions for a reasonable price; and even this is an exertion of power, which the legislature indulges with caution, and which nothing but the legislature can perform.[43]

Blackstone was anxious to support the principle that property is an "absolute right, inherent in every Englishman."[44] Thus, he wrote immediately before the passage quoted above, "the law permits no man, or set of men [to take land] without consent of the owner of the land."[45] In order to preserve this principle that no property can be taken without consent, Blackstone insisted that all takings had to be authorized by Parliament, thereby providing constructive consent through representation. But Blackstone went further, construing the compensation requirement as a manifestation of the

43. BLACKSTONE, *supra* note 22, at *135 (emphasis added).

44. *Id.* at *134.

45. *Id.* at *135.

principle that "[t]he public is now considered as an individual, treating with an individual for an exchange." In other words, in order to take property, the sovereign must step down into the marketplace, and deal with the owner on terms of an exchange of equivalents. By forcing the sovereign to give "full indemnification and equivalent" for the value of the land taken, we thus preserve the principle that even the sovereign must respect the inviolability of property rights.

In Blackstone's account, then, the purpose of requiring compensation is to maintain the vertical balance of power between sovereign and subject, and in particular, to prevent the government from oppressing rights of private property. It is perhaps not too fanciful to say that Blackstone anticipates the "fiscal illusion" and "process failure" theories of compensation which have come to the fore in recent years, and to which we turn in the next chapter.

It would be hazardous, however, to attribute the particular views of either the natural law thinkers or of Blackstone to the Framers of the Constitution. The discussions of the power of eminent domain found in the natural law treatises, and Blackstone's favorable comments about the English practice of compensating for takings of property, help us to understand why the founding generation regarded the Takings Clause with such equanimity. But there is nothing in the historical record that specifically links the views of these commentators with the participants in the framing of the Bill of Rights.

The truth is that no one who participated in the drafting and ratification of the Takings Clause—including James Madison, who bears the most responsibility for the Clause—had given any sustained thought to the purposes of eminent domain and the compensation requirement. The understanding of these purposes remained to be worked out over time.

CHAPTER III

MODERN THEORIES OF THE TAKINGS CLAUSE

Given the paucity of evidence about why the Framers adopted the Takings Clause, scholars have attempted to fill the gap with a variety of normative theories not grounded in original intent. These efforts raise a number of far-reaching questions about the proper relationship between the individual and the state, and are of interest in their own right. Yet there is also a pragmatic reason to gain some familiarity with these theories. The writings of Joseph Sax, Frank Michelman, Richard Epstein, and others have had a discernible influence on the courts as they have struggled to resolve difficult issues presented by the Takings Clause. Thus, in this area at least, someone who has no ambition beyond understanding the evolution of legal doctrine needs to know something about legal theory.

Academic theories of the takings problem, especially in recent years, tend to pose the inquiry in broad terms. They ask, in effect: When, if ever, should the government compensate individuals whose expectations have been frustrated by legal change?[46] In order to keep our inquiry focused on

46. For notable examples, *see* DANIEL SHAVIRO, WHEN RULES CHANGE: AN ECONOMIC AND POLITICAL ANALYSIS OF TRANSITION RELIEF

the Takings Clause, we will break the discussion down into three more specific sets of issues: (1) Why does the government have the power to engage in forced exchanges of property rights? (2) Why do we generally require the government to pay just compensation when it exercises this power? (3) Why do we sometimes permit the government to interfere with property rights without paying compensation, that is, what is the proper scope and function of the police power?

A. The Rationale for Forced Exchange

As noted in Chapter II, natural law theorists of the Seventeenth and Eighteenth Centuries disagreed about the permissible ends of the power of eminent domain. Some argued that it should be limited to cases of strict necessity; others, that it should be available more widely to promote public welfare. But none of these early writers had any explanation for why the government would want to compel the transfer of property rights in the first place. Most of the time, the government acquires the specific resources it needs through voluntary purchase. This is true not only with respect to labor services, perishable commodities, and tangible personal property like vehicles, but also with respect to land and buildings. Given that government can

AND RETROACTIVITY (2000); Louis Kaplow, *An Economic Analysis of Legal Transitions*, 99 HARV. L. REV. 509, 576–80 (1986). Both works treat the takings issue as one species of a larger family of problems that includes also changes in tax and liability rules.

usually get by with voluntary exchange, why do we sometimes allow it to do what ordinary individuals cannot—take someone's property without his or her consent?

Modern transaction-costs economics has significantly advanced our understanding of the rationale for eminent domain.[47] As long as the government faces a "thick" market, *i.e.*, a market where many persons are offering to sell a given resource, it does not need to engage in forced exchange. If one seller balks or holds out for an excessive price, the government can simply turn to another. Thus, where markets are reasonably thick—as is the case with most markets for personal services, commodities, and personal property, and is sometimes the case with respect to markets for land or buildings—there is no need to use the power of eminent domain.

Things change, however, when the government seeks to acquire resources in a thin market—in the extreme case, in a market in which there is only one potential seller. Such a seller has monopoly power vis-à-vis the government, and may hold out for a price far in excess of the seller's opportunity cost (the price the seller could get for the resource in any other application). If the government is forced

47. For early recognition of the economic explanation, *see* Richard A. Posner, Economic Analysis of Law 21–24 (1st ed. 1972); Patricia Munch, *An Economic Analysis of Eminent Domain*, 84 J. Pol. Econ. 473, 473–80 (1976); Guido Calabresi & A. Douglas Melamed, *Property Rules, Liability Rules, and Inalienability: One View of the Cathedral*, 85 Harv. L. Rev. 1089 (1972). The account here follows Thomas W. Merrill, *The Economics of Public Use*, 72 Cornell L. Rev. 61, 74–77 (1986).

to rely on voluntary exchange in these circumstances, bargaining may break down, or the government (and ultimately the taxpayers) may have to pay an exorbitant price for the resource. By giving the government the power to compel transfers of property, the government can compel any seller with monopoly power to convey the resource in return for compensation equal to its opportunity cost, that is, at a price stripped of any monopoly pricing component associated with the government project. The project can thus go forward without undue delay or burden on taxpayers.

Consider two examples of how the government may find itself confronted with a monopoly seller of resources. Suppose the government decides to create a memorial park at the site of the Battle of Gettysburg, but part of the battlefield site is in private hands.[48] The landowner is, in effect, a monopoly supplier of a key resource for which there is no alternative source of supply. As a monopolist, the landowner is in a position to charge monopoly prices to the government. The opportunity cost of the land—what the landowner could obtain for it in any other application, such as selling to a local farmer—may be fairly modest, say $10,000. But given the government's project and its lack of options in finding another source, the landowner can charge much more, say $50,000. The difference—$40,000 in our example—is a "monopoly rent," a

48. This, in fact, was the situation in one of the first litigated cases involving the use of eminent domain by the federal government. *See* United States v. Gettysburg Elec. R. Co., 160 U.S. 668 (1896).

return above and beyond the landowner's opportunity cost. Eminent domain offers a solution to this kind of monopoly problem. If the government condemns the land, it can acquire a needed resource without providing a windfall to the landowner or without imposing an undue burden on taxpayers.

A more typical example arises when the government or its delegate wishes to construct a highway, railroad, or fiber optic cable from point A to point B. To do so, it must acquire rights in a strip of land (either a fee simple or an easement) that roughly follows a line from A to B. This means that every person who owns land along the proposed route has a monopoly on a key asset—one portion of the continuous strip of land needed to obtain the right of way. Given the imperative of assembling numerous contiguous strips of land together to form the right of way, each landowner is in a position to extract monopoly rents from the government in return for selling his or her portion of the right of way, just as the owner of the battlefield site was in the previous example. Using eminent domain to acquire the needed right of way from owners who hold out has the same effect here as in the case of the battlefield site owner: It eliminates windfalls to landowners, and avoids imposing excessive costs on taxpayers.

A similar analysis can be made of other uses of eminent domain, whether it be for acquiring sites for cellular radio transmission towers, imposing conservation easements on a tract of ecologically sensitive land, or obtaining rights to a patent that is blocking further progress in a research program. In each case, the power is needed to acquire some resource that is critical to completing a government program or objective—critical in the sense that there are no good substitutes. This rationale for eminent domain has gone essentially unchallenged since it was first advanced. It represents an important, if small, instance of true progress in understanding the takings problem.

Note, however, that the monopoly explanation for why the government needs the power of forced exchange raises some further questions. The government is obviously not the only entity that faces problems of monopoly sellers when it acquires resources.[49] Virtually every real estate developer confronts this problem to some degree, as does every individual who has ever coveted a particular house or antique owned by someone who is not interested in selling. Should we limit the power of forced exchange to the government? Or should the power be made more generally available? Are there hidden dangers that counsel in favor of limiting the use of

49. It has been observed that the law often shifts from "property rules" (exclusion rights) to "liability rules" (forced exchange with compensation) in high-transaction-cost situations. *See* Calabresi & Melamed, *supra* note 47. In this sense, the scope of the power of eminent domain is part of a broader debate over how far the law should go in substituting liability rules for property rules. *Compare* Ian Ayres & J.M. Balkin, *Legal Entitlements as Auctions: Property Rules, Liability Rules, and Beyond*, 106 YALE L.J. 703 (1996) (endorsing innovative uses of liability rules) *with* Richard A. Epstein, *A Clear View of the Cathedral: The Dominance of Property Rules*, 106 YALE L. REV. 2091 (1996) (arguing that liability rules should be carefully cabined).

this power to the government and a few other types of entities like common carriers and public utilities? These questions will be discussed further in Chapter VIII when we consider the public use limitation.

B. The Rationale for Compensation

If the rationale for allowing the government to engage in forced exchange of property is to overcome problems associated with monopoly, why do we generally require the government to pay just compensation when it engages in such forced transfers? Why not allow the government to take needed assets without paying, or at least give the government discretion in setting the amount of compensation it decides to pay?

In contrast to our first question—why permit forced exchange at all?—no clear consensus has been reached as to why the government should compensate for takings. Three general types of justifications have been advanced in support of a compensation requirement, which we will call the "equal treatment," "fiscal illusion," and "process failure" arguments. Although scholars have disagreed among themselves about which of these is the "true" rationale for the compensation requirement, the justifications are not incompatible in many respects. Takings theory in this regard resembles tort theory. Tort scholars argue among themselves over whether the rationale for awarding damages for torts is to provide compensation to victims, to deter undesirable behavior by perpetrators, or to provide corrective justice as between victim and perpetrator. Perhaps it is all three. In other words, it is possible that the tort system has multiple, mutually supporting rationales.[50] Similarly, it may be that the practice of providing compensation for government takings of property has multiple rationales, and that these rationales are stronger in the aggregate than any one rationale would be in isolation.

1. *Equal Treatment*

As we saw in Chapter II, natural law theorists believed that compensation is required when the government takes property in order "to even the score when a given person has been required to give up property rights beyond his just share of the cost of government."[51] The idea that compensation is required in order to restore individuals whose property has been taken to a position of parity with their fellow citizens we call the equal treatment justification. It bears a clear resemblance to the theory of tort law that emphasizes the importance of compensating victims of accidents that are no fault of their own.

The equal treatment justification remains today the most widespread explanation for the compensa-

50. *See* Gary T. Schwartz, *Mixed Theories of Tort Law: Affirming Both Deterrence and Corrective Justice*, 75 TEX. L. REV. 1801 (1997).

51. William B. Stoebuck, *A General Theory of Eminent Domain*, 47 WASH. L. REV. 553, 587 (1972) (summarizing the views of natural law scholars).

tion requirement. The Supreme Court has often repeated that the purpose of the Takings Clause is to bar government "from forcing some people alone to bear public burdens which, in all fairness and justice, should be borne by the public as a whole."[52] The difficulty, of course, comes in specifying more precisely when a burden on isolated individuals becomes so disproportionate that it violates our sense of "fairness and justice."

In routine exercises of eminent domain, application of the equal treatment rationale is relatively straightforward. Suppose the government must acquire a right of way across 50 contiguous tracts of land in order to construct a highway from points A to B. Forty-nine owners agree voluntarily to sell. The fiftieth holds out, forcing the government to resort to eminent domain. According to the equal treatment rationale, the government should pay just compensation to the fiftieth owner in order to put that owner in roughly the same position as other similarly situated owners. Otherwise, the landowner whose property is taken by eminent domain will have to pay a disproportionate share of the common costs of government relative to other owners who either did not have their property taken or voluntary sold their interest to the government.

52. Armstrong v. United States, 364 U.S. 40, 49 (1960). For a review of the popularity of this quotation in takings cases and literature, *see* William Michael Treanor, *The Armstrong Principle, The Narratives of Takings, and Compensation Statutes*, 38 WM. & MARY L. REV. 1151 (1997).

When we move beyond the routine eminent domain case, however, it becomes more difficult to say when fairness and justice require compensation in order to preserve the principle of equal treatment. In particular, what if the government does not take title to property, but merely adopts a regulation that has the effect of diminishing the value of one or a few persons' property? Should compensation be paid in all or some of these cases, and if so, which ones?

The most complete exploration of the equal treatment idea is the now-classic article by Frank Michelman,[53] who sought to develop a more systematic justification for the compensation requirement by drawing upon utilitarian moral theory and John Rawls' theory of justice.[54] Michelman introduced the concept of "demoralization costs," which he defined as the costs associated with any government action that causes property owners to experience uncompensated losses. Such costs, he maintained, include not only the psychological pain incurred by losers and their sympathizers from uncompensated losses, but also the forgone investment caused by fear of such losses on the part of property owners more generally. Michelman recognized that demoralization costs should not be reduced to zero by compensating for all losses. Instead, he argued, the

---

53. Frank I. Michelman, *Property, Utility, and Fairness: Comments on the Ethical Foundations of "Just Compensation" Law*, 80 HARV. L. REV. 1165 (1967).

54. Michelman's article preceded the publication of Rawls's book, *see* JOHN RAWLS, A THEORY OF JUSTICE (1971), but relied on earlier articles that Rawls had written.

government should compensate only when demoralization costs exceed what he called "settlement costs"—the costs of paying compensation and of administering a compensation system. Both demoralization costs and settlement costs are real costs to society—they represent forgone resources that could be used for other purposes. Michelman suggested that the objective should be to minimize the costs associated with government action that impairs property values, by incurring either settlement costs or demoralization costs, whichever is less.

Michelman's framework provides an explanation for why compensation is routinely paid for formal takings by eminent domain and permanent physical invasions, but not for most regulations of the use of property. Formal condemnations and permanent physical invasions will ordinarily impose high demoralization costs, because they deprive the owner of all of the value associated with property. Moreover, such events are relatively easy to identify and admit of objective measurement in terms of lost value, thus reducing the settlement costs associated with administering a compensation system for such losses. In contrast, when we turn to regulations that have some negative impact on property values, demoralization costs will generally be smaller, because only part of the value is taken. At the same time, the settlement costs of identifying affected owners and determining the proper amount of compensation will often be relatively high, especially if the regulation affects a substantial number of owners.

Michelman offered a number of other observations about why compensation is not required for all types of government action that adversely affect property values. He pointed out that government policies broadly designed to produce a more equal distribution of wealth, such as progressive taxes and welfare programs, are not subject to compensation requirements.[55] He suggested that this is because general measures that are designed to equalize the distribution of wealth are not perceived by most people as being unjust and unfair. He also noted that if we extend our horizons beyond a single challenged action to look at a series of government actions over time, losses by a property owner on one occasion will often be offset by gains on other occasions, thereby eliminating any unequal treatment.[56] Finally, he pointed out that some regulations are designed merely to rectify past actions in which one party has diminished the value of another's property, *e.g.*, by creating a nuisance. No compensation is required in these cases to preserve equal treatment because the regulation simply restores the status quo that existed before the nuisance was perpetrated.[57]

Even after all these adjustments are made, however, Michelman acknowledged that his theory would seem to require a much more wide-ranging compensation practice than the one we have today. In particular, any regulation of property that visits

55. Michelman, *supra* note 53, at 1181–82.

56. *Id.* at 1225.

57. *Id.* at 1235–37.

large and unanticipated costs on a discrete group of owners would appear to warrant compensation, provided the regulation is not designed to rectify some past disruption of the status quo. Michelman surmised that the reason compensation is so limited is that courts lack the capacity to engage in inquiries requiring extensive information about things like demoralization and settlement costs. Thus, they must rely on relatively formalistic rules of decision to keep decisional costs at a manageable level.[58] Given the underinclusiveness of current compensation practices from an equal treatment perspective, however, Michelman urged that legislatures develop administrative compensation schemes to complement the limited judicial scheme that exists under the Takings Clause.[59]

Michelman's equal treatment theory, with its emphasis on demoralization costs, is vulnerable to one important objection. Compensation, in Michelman's scheme, performs roughly the same function as mandatory insurance against the taking of property by the government.[60] But property values are exposed to risks from all sorts of calamities, ranging from fire to flood to theft, each of which gives rise to demoralization costs. In most instances, however, there is no right to government compensation for such casualties; certainly, there is no right to com-

58. *Id.* at 1245–56.

59. *Id.* at 1253–56.

60. *See* William A. Fischel & Perry Shapiro, *Takings, Insurance, and Michelman: Comments on Economic Interpretation of "Just Compensation" Law*, 17 J. LEGAL STUD. 269 (1988); Kaplow, *supra* note 46, at 533–36.

pensation guaranteed by the Constitution. Instead, we leave it to owners to purchase private insurance or otherwise take measures to manage the risk of loss, such as through diversification of holdings. Michelman's equal treatment theory thus calls for some explanation why we need compulsory government insurance for takings, when we get by with private insurance with respect to other losses.

Michelman offered one possible distinction between takings and other types of casualities: Takings result from a deliberate decision by political majorities to take the property of a minority.[61] Michelman suggested that this kind of deliberate majoritarian action is uniquely demoralizing—more demoralizing than acts of God (like fires and floods) or deliberate depredations by isolated individuals (like theft). But this psychological generalization is debatable. Takings are usually designed to produce important community benefits. Realizing this, people might be less demoralized by a taking than by losses inflicted by natural disaster or theft, which seems random and unjustified. And even if it is true that takings are especially demoralizing, it would seem that if the demoralization is greater, people would have more incentive to purchase insurance against this risk, making government intervention less rather than more imperative.

Other commentators have suggested that compulsory government insurance may be required because takings give rise to special problems of moral hazard and adverse selection that would prevent

61. Michelman, *supra* note 53, at 1165–66.

the emergence of a private insurance market.[62] Moral hazard exists when insured persons can affect the probability that an insurable event will occur. Since takings are the outcome of the political process, and the political process is open to influence by affected citizens, property owners may be in a position to affect the probability that their property will be taken. Persons with insurance might offer less resistance to takings than persons without insurance, which would make private insurance companies reluctant to insure against this risk.

Adverse selection exists when insured persons have superior knowledge of the probability that an insurable event will occur. Because takings are the outcome of the political process, some property owners may have inside information about whether their property is likely to be taken. Owners who believe their property is more likely to be taken are more likely to purchase insurance. This too could make private insurance companies reluctant to provide coverage.

Other commentators have expressed skepticism about whether moral hazard and adverse selection are significantly greater problems with respect to takings than other insurable risks associated with actions by human agents, such as professional malpractice or breach of fiduciary duty.[63] The issue

62. *See* Lawrence Blume & Daniel L. Rubinfeld, *Compensation for Takings: An Economic Analysis*, 72 CAL. L. REV. 569, 592–97 (1984).

63. *See, e.g.,* Kaplow, *supra* note 46, at 536–50; Daniel A. Farber, *Public Choice and Just Compensation*, 9 CONST. COMMENT. 279, 284 (1992).

remains unresolved. Unless it can be demonstrated that mandatory government insurance is necessary because of some failure in private insurance markets, the equal treatment justification will remain less than a fully satisfactory explanation for why we look to the government for compensation when it engages in forced exchange.[64]

2. *Fiscal Illusion*

The second general justification for the compensation requirement shifts the focus from fairness to efficiency. The argument here is that compensation is required in order to internalize the costs of takings of property to the government.[65] Takings entail not only demoralization costs, but also oppor-

64. Some confirmation of the market failure hypothesis is provided by the market for insurance against expropriation of foreign investments. Although private insurance against foreign expropriation has been available from time to time through Lloyd's of London, the primary source of protection since the early 1970s has been insurance purchased from the Overseas Private Investment Corporation, a public entity. *See* Maura B. Perry, *A Model for Efficient Foreign Aid: The Case for the Political Risk Insurance Activities of the Overseas Private Investment Corporation*, 36 VA. J. INT. L. 511 (1996). Public insurance appears to outperform private insurance in this market in part because a public insurer can engage in more widespread diversification of risk, and in part because a public insurer can use its political influence to reduce the incidence of loss. *See id.* at 551–57. In other words, public insurance does a better job of reducing problems of adverse selection and moral hazard.

65. *See* RICHARD A. POSNER, ECONOMIC ANALYSIS OF LAW 64 (5th ed. 1998); Jack L. Knetsch & Thomas E. Borcherding, *Expropriation of Private Property and the Basis for Compensation*, 29 U. TORONTO L.J. 237, 242–44 (1979).

tunity costs. Once the government takes property, the owner cannot put it to any alternative use. By requiring the government to pay compensation for assets taken, the argument goes, we force government officials to compare the value of the resource in government hands to its value in private use. Presumably, officials will go forward with the taking only if they anticipate that the resource will produce greater value as part of the government project than the compensation the government must pay to obtain it. If we do not require the government to pay compensation for takings, in contrast, government officials may suffer from the "fiscal illusion" that the resources they take have no opportunity cost. As a result, they may engage in excessive takings of property, resulting in a misallocation of resources.[66]

If the equal treatment justification is the analogue of the compensation rationale for awards of damages in tort theory, then the fiscal illusion argument is the analogue of the deterrence rationale. The deterrence rationale in tort shifts the focus from the victim to the perpetrator. By forcing the perpetrator of the tort to pay damages to the victim, the law causes the perpetrator to internalize the costs of the accident. This creates an incentive to potential perpetrators to take efficient precautions to avoid injuries to future victims in similar circumstances. The fiscal illusion argument makes a similar point about compensation for takings, with

66. *See* Michael A. Heller & James E. Krier, *Deterrence and Distribution in the Law of Takings*, 112 HARV. L. REV. 997, 999 (1999).

the government now playing the role of perpetrator. By forcing the government to pay just compensation when it takes property, we cause the government to internalize the costs of engaging in forced transfers of property rights. This creates an incentive for the government to limit its use of forced exchange to circumstances in which it is efficient to do so, that is, where the benefits to the public exceed the opportunity costs of using the resource for some other purpose.

The fiscal illusion argument is almost certainly correct as applied to the acquisition of conventional assets that are bought and sold in the marketplace. Suppose, for example, that the government were permitted to requisition office supplies from manufacturers without paying compensation for them. Such a rule would almost certainly lead to large stockpiles of pens and paperclips in government offices, not to mention a rather casual attitude toward government employees taking pens and paperclips home for their personal use. This overuse of office supplies by the government would have an opportunity cost—the cartons of pens and paperclips sitting idle in government supply rooms could be used by other persons for more productive purposes. But government officials would be unlikely to perceive this opportunity cost very clearly.[67] Requiring that the government compensate for office supplies taken thus yields a more efficient allocation of resources than would prevail if the government

67. Of course, if the government is a major consumer of the item relative to the nongovernmental market, as for example with military aircraft, then the policy of requisitioning without compensation would presumably drive all potential sellers out of

could take office supplies for free.

The fiscal illusion theory has one clear advantage over the equal treatment theory: It can explain why private insurance is not the answer to government takings. If takings were covered by private insurance, the costs of inefficient government stockpiling of resources would still be externalized to nongovernmental actors, rather than being internalized by the government.[68] Even though the costs might be spread more widely through private insurance premiums, they would still be an externality from the government's perspective. The analogy to the tort system is again instructive. Requiring property owners to insure against government takings would be like eliminating liability for torts and requiring that all compensation be made through first-party (no-fault) insurance. This might reduce risk and spread losses, but it would do so at the cost of eliminating incentives to avoid inefficient accident-causing behavior.

On the other hand, the fiscal illusion theory is vulnerable to a different objection, namely, that the cost-internalization story operates in two directions.[69] Not only do we want government officials

the market. In this instance, the government would have to pay for the product voluntarily or make the product itself.

68. Unless perhaps the insurer could sue the government for indemnification. We assume, given standard limitations on government tort liability, that this would not happen.

69. Kaplow, *supra* note 46, at 531; Lawrence Blume et al., *The Taking of Land: When Should Compensation be Paid?*, 99 Q.J. Econ. 71, 90–91 (1984).

to have efficient incentives to regulate, we also want private parties to have efficient incentives to desist from activity that warrants regulation. If all declines in property values associated with government regulation result in compensation, then this will eliminate the deterrent effect to engaging in activity subject to government regulation. For example, if the government must compensate the owner of a factory shut down for polluting, this obviously undermines the incentive effects of rules prohibiting pollution. Assuming that much, if not most, regulated activity has a negative net social value, then compensating for regulatory losses would create perverse incentives to engage in antisocial behavior.

As this objection reveals, the concern about fiscal illusion is simply a species of a more general concern about limiting behavior that imposes external costs on others. Once we see that this is the case, the fiscal illusion argument becomes vastly more complicated. We want to create incentives for the government to behave efficiently, but we also want to create incentives for private parties to behave efficiently. Adopting a regime of cost-internalization for the government will undermine cost-internalization by private parties; conversely, adopting a regime of cost-internalization for private parties sacrifices cost-internalization by the government. In theory, decisionmakers might be able to figure out which effect is dominant in any particular case. But the information costs of doing so would be so daunting that it is unrealistic to expect the courts to do the calculus. As Michelman recognized with respect to the balancing of demoralization costs and settlement costs, courts will have to rely on rough-and-ready rules that rest on generalizations about which effect is likely to be more important in different circumstances.

3. Process Failure

A third group of theories grounds the compensation requirement in the need to overcome certain failures of the political process. The central problem of the political process emphasized by these theories is that different interest groups have different degrees of influence in a democratic political system.[70] The degree of influence of any group depends not only on the number of voters that it represents, but also on other factors, such as the costs of organizing the group and how many resources the group controls. As a consequence, political outcomes in a democracy do not reflect any neat summation of individual preferences. Rather, outcomes will be systematically skewed in favor of the preferences of those groups with disproportionate influence.

The problem of differential influence has spawned a number of ideas about why government should compensate for takings of property. One interesting suggestion is that compensation functions as an

[70]. This is commonly referred to as the interest group theory of politics, a subset of public choice theory. For an introduction, *see* DANIEL A FARBER & PHILIP P. FRICKEY, LAW AND PUBLIC CHOICE: A CRITICAL INTRODUCTION 12–37 (1991); MANCUR OLSON, THE LOGIC OF COLLECTIVE ACTION (1965).

important element in overcoming the opposition of intense minorities to projects that are in the interest of the diffuse majority.[71] Suppose there is a proposal to take the land of ten property owners for use as a public park. The park would provide small but significant benefits to thousands of people, and these benefits would, in the aggregate, exceed the opportunity costs and demoralization costs associated with a seizure of the land without compensation. Nevertheless, compensating the property owners for the value of their land may still be a good idea if we want to see the park created. This is because the ten property owners are likely to exert differential influence in the decisionmaking process; certainly, it will be easier for them to organize in opposition to the park than it will be for the thousands of beneficiaries to organize in its support. Providing an advance guarantee of compensation for such takings will soften the opposition of the losers to a considerable degree. Thus, compensation may be an important tool in assuring that governmental projects supported by a diffuse majority are not scuttled by intense minorities.

This "buyoff" theory, in contrast to the equal treatment and fiscal illusion theories, seems to suggest that current compensation practices are too broad. It may suggest, for example, that although a moderate-sized group capable of forming significant opposition to a project should receive compensation

71. *See* Glynn S. Lunney, Jr., *A Critical Reexamination of the Takings Jurisprudence*, 90 MICH. L. REV. 1892, 1954–63 (1992); Farber, *supra* note 63, at 289–90; Saul Levmore, *Just Compensation and Just Politics*, 22 CONN. L. REV. 285, 305–19 (1990).

for takings, one person or a group too small or powerless to exert any political influence should receive no compensation. Perhaps because this result seems especially unfair, the buyoff theory has been endorsed only in qualified form.[72]

Another theory is that differential influence is more of a problem at some levels of the political system than at other levels, and hence that protections against takings should vary with the level of government that perpetrates the taking. William Fischel, in particular, has argued that the problem of differential influence is likely to be a serious one at the local level, where, for example, existing property owners may seek to freeze out new development or to impose disproportionate costs on newcomers in the form of exactions on new development of property.[73] This is because existing landowners are usually a well-organized and vocal interest in the local community, whereas newcomers seeking to relocate to the community are probably poorly represented. At the other extreme, all relevant interests are likely to be represented when the federal government sets policy affecting property rights, making skewed outcomes less likely. Fischel therefore proposes that courts give the greatest scrutiny to alleged takings by local governments, intermediate scrutiny to alleged takings by state governments, and the most deferential

72. *See, e.g.,* Farber, *supra* note 63, at 287–94; Levmore, *supra* note 71, at 306–11.

73. WILLIAM A. FISCHEL, REGULATORY TAKINGS: LAW, ECONOMICS, AND POLITICS 100–40, 341–42 (1995). Exactions are described and discussed in greater detail *infra* Chapter IX.

scrutiny to alleged takings by the federal government.[74]

Fischel's emphasis on differential influence at the local and state level has been criticized for downplaying the role of competition among local and state governments, which may constrain these governments from deviating too far from policies that would be optimal from the perspective of the aggregate interest.[75] For example, local communities are interested not only in placating existing homeowners, but also in attracting new jobs and tax dollars. If one community imposes too high a price for permitting new development, developers will turn to another community willing to offer better terms. The threat of developers and employers "voting with their feet" keeps local authorities from capitulating to groups like existing homeowners. The debate over whether this kind of regulatory competition effectively counteracts differential influence at the local and state level is complex, and so far unresolved.

A third theory, which has been advanced by Richard Epstein, is by far the most ambitious conception of the compensation requirement.[76] Epstein starts with the assumption that groups with differential influence continually engage in rent-seeking behav-

74. *Id*. at 100–40.

75. *See* Vicki Been, *"Exit" as a Constraint on Land Use Exactions: Rethinking the Unconstitutional Conditions Doctrine*, 91 COLUM. L. REV. 473, 506–28 (1991).

76. RICHARD A. EPSTEIN, TAKINGS: PRIVATE PROPERTY AND THE POWER OF EMINENT DOMAIN (1985).

ior, that is, they try to use state power to enrich themselves at the expense of others. This they do by lobbying for tax breaks, for regulations that burden competitors, and for new liability rules that transfer wealth to themselves from others. Epstein argues that we should construe the Takings Clause as requiring the payment of just compensation whenever a person experiences a decline in property values because of changes in rules of taxation, regulation, or liability, unless it can be shown that implicit compensation has been provided or the police power exception applies. Such a rule would in effect nullify any advantage from using the power of the state to enrich one group at the expense of others. The state could no longer be used as an instrument for wealth redistribution. Only positive sum games would go forward; zero sum or negative sum games would be checked by a universal compensation requirement.

Epstein's anti-rent-seeking theory yields a Takings Clause of cosmic proportions, and has elicited a barrage of opposition.[77] The most common objection is that his theory would make it unconstitutional for the government to engage in any form of progressive taxation or to provide welfare benefits to the poor. This is contrary to the general assumption, noted by Michelman, that general laws designed to equalize the distribution of wealth fall

77. *See, e.g.,* Symposium, *Richard Epstein's Takings: Private Property and the Power of Eminent Domain*, 41 U. MIAMI L. REV. 1 (1986); Mark Kelman, *Taking Takings Seriously: An Essay for Centrists*, 74 CAL. L. REV. 1829 (1986) (book review); Joseph L. Sax, *Takings*, 53 U. CHI. L. REV. 279 (1986) (book review).

outside the scope of the Takings Clause. Another objection is that Epstein's universal compensation requirement would entail a vastly expanded role for the judiciary, exceeding its capacity to process cases and its competence to dissect the economic impact of various regulatory and tax measures. At a minimum, Epstein's anti-redistribution theory, like Michelman's equal treatment theory and the fiscal illusion theory, would have to be reduced to decisional rules that demand less processing of information by judges.[78]

Although no consensus has been reached about which of these theories provides the best justification for the compensation requirement, it is important to note that the theories are, in many respects, mutually supportive. Each of the theories would require compensation for traditional exercises of eminent domain by local authorities, and each would require no compensation for regulations that prohibit factories from emitting harmful pollutants. The theories present more divergent implications about where to draw the line between these polar cases. But it is also noteworthy that many of the theories suggest that the costs of finetuning the inquiry in borderline cases is likely to entail an excessive burden for courts. Thus, the theories are

---

78. Epstein, to his credit, does seek to develop more concrete decisional rules to implement his general anti-redistribution principle, for example, in specifying when government action provides "implicit in-kind compensation" and when government action falls within the police power (see next subsection). Even so, these rules would often require courts to develop unfamiliar economic testimony that they are probably not competent to assess.

also mutually supportive in suggesting that there is a need to develop rules of decision that serve as proxies for the underlying considerations in determining when compensation is appropriate.

C. The Scope of the Police Power

Courts have long recognized that compensation is not required if the government action constitutes a legitimate exercise of the police power as opposed to the power of eminent domain. Although history provides some guidance as to what kinds of regulations fall within the police power, the concept is inherently vague and its scope has been the subject of almost continuous dispute. Not surprisingly, therefore, commentators have also attempted to develop theories that would provide more coherent guidance in determining the proper domain of the police power.

Perhaps the most influential effort along these lines is the work of Joseph Sax. In an early article, Sax argued that the line between takings and the police power should turn on whether government is acting as an enterprise or as a mediator.[79] When the government competes for resources with other potential users—for example, when it acquires land for a highway or post office—it acts as an enterprise and must pay compensation. However, when the government settles a conflict between private claim-

79. Joseph L. Sax, *Takings and the Police Power*, 74 YALE L.J. 36, 62–63 (1964).

ants to a resource—as when it adopts a zoning ordinance that prohibits operating a brickyard in a residential neighborhood—then it acts as mediator and does not need to pay compensation. This enterprise/mediation distinction suggests that the line between eminent domain and the police power is crossed when the government goes beyond resolving land use conflicts and instead seeks to dedicate a resource to the general benefit of the public, as when it prohibits the filling of a wetland that is a habitat for migrating waterfowl or the modification of an historic building.[80]

In a later article, Sax broadened the concept of mediation to include any government action that regulates a use of property that has a spillover effect.[81] In this revised account, the police power encompasses any government regulation designed to minimize negative externalities or promote positive externalities associated with the use of property. This revision allowed Sax to sweep nearly all environmental and conservation measures into the police power category. In particular, government efforts to secure the public benefits associated with wetlands or historic preservation now fall on the police power side of the line. Unfortunately, Sax's revised definition of the police power is so broad that it might even include some traditional exercises of the power of eminent domain. Nearly all uses

80. *See id.* at 72–73 (acknowledging that the government acts as an enterprise when it adopts a regulation prohibiting development of a wetland).

81. Joseph L. Sax, *Takings, Private Property, and Public Rights*, 81 YALE L.J. 149 (1971).

of property have some spillover effects, either positive or negative. At a minimum, Sax's revised view would appear to operate as a rule that no regulation that falls short of a complete appropriation of property ever requires the payment of compensation.

Richard Epstein has also advanced a theory of the police power to go along with his anti-rent-seeking theory of the compensation requirement. For Epstein, the police power is a shorthand reference for the state's power to assist individuals in defending their private property against tortious interferences by others.[82] As he puts it, "the wrong of the citizen justifies conduct otherwise wrongful by the state as representative of and in defense of its other citizens."[83] In practical terms, this means the police power for Epstein is coterminous with the power of individual property owners to obtain legal relief against nuisances. Furthermore, Epstein rejects a broad conception of nuisance, such as the *Restatement of Torts'* definition of a nuisance as any intentional activity in which the gravity of the harm outweighs the utility of the defendant's conduct.[84] Instead, he would restrict nuisances to activities that cause harm through some physical invasion of the plaintiff's land, as by smoke, noise or vibrations. Given these limitations, Epstein would exclude wet-

82. EPSTEIN, *supra* note 76, at 107–25.

83. *Id.* at 111.

84. *See* RESTATEMENT (SECOND) OF TORTS § 826 (defining the unreasonable conduct that constitutes an actionable intentional nuisance).

land and historic preservation measures from the scope of the police power.[85]

Epstein's reasons for limiting the police power to nuisance regulation, and for limiting nuisances to physical invasions, are not clearly spelled out. It appears, however, that he is attracted to the bright line quality of these limitations because they will limit legislative and regulatory struggles over the appropriate scope of the police power exception. In effect, his advocacy of a formalistic definition of the police power is part and parcel of his more general project to limit the ability of groups with differential influence to use the political process to secure redistributions of wealth.

The debate between Sax and Epstein over the scope of the police power can be related to our earlier discussion of the equal treatment and fiscal illusion theories for the compensation requirement. We noted that both of these theories run into problems of judicial implementation as they extend beyond traditional exercises of eminent domain to include various types of government regulation of property. At some point, settlement costs exceed demoralization costs, and at some point, the gains from requiring cost-internalization by property owners exceed the gains from requiring cost-internalization by the government. But courts lack the

85. EPSTEIN, *supra* note 76, at 123. Epstein's theory of nuisance liability is spelled out more fully in Richard A. Epstein, *Nuisance Law: Corrective Justice and its Utilitarian Constraints*, 8 J. LEGAL STUD. 49 (1979).

tools to determine when the lines cross with any precision.

The search for a definition of the police power reflected in the work of Sax and Epstein can be seen as an effort to identify a proxy that can be used by courts to identify the approximate point where the benefits of compensation no longer exceed the costs. Sax proposes a definition that cuts off compensation very close to formal exercises in eminent domain; in effect, he believes that settlement costs quickly exceed demoralization costs and/or that cost-internalization by private parties is more important than cost-internalization by the government. Epstein proposes a definition that would cut off compensation at a considerable distance from formal exercises of eminent domain; his intuition is that demoralization costs often exceed settlement costs and/or that it is more important to assure cost-internalization by the government than by private property owners.

Who is right about the relative benefits and costs of compensation, and hence about the proper definition of the police power for courts to use as a proxy in limiting the compensation requirement? The ultimate point of dispute here may boil down to whether we believe the government is capable of transcending the self-seeking nature of the individuals it represents.[86] Obviously, people have different intuitions about how much goodness we can expect from government. Sax believes that the government

86. *See* Thomas W. Merrill, *Rent Seeking and the Compensation Principle*, 80 Nw. U. L. Rev. 1561, 1586–89 (1986).

generally acts in the public interest, and hence should have broad leeway to regulate property uses without having to pay compensation. Epstein, in contrast, is deeply pessimistic about the prospects for collective altruism. Accordingly, he would require compensation whenever the government ventures beyond nuisance regulation, narrowly defined. Hence we see that takings theory is ultimately about political theory—specifically, about how much faith one has in government.

Chapter IV

Private Property

In order to invoke the Takings Clause, a claimant must show that (1) his or her "private property" (2) has been "taken" by the government (3) for a "public use" (4) without "just compensation." The language of the Clause thus suggests four distinct legal requirements must be satisfied in order to make out a constitutional violation: private property, government taking, public use, and the absence of just compensation. The next five chapters examine each of these requirements in more detail. We begin in this chapter with private property. Chapters V and VI turn to the takings requirement. Chapter VII considers just compensation. Chapter VIII evaluates the public use element.

The threshold requirement in any takings case is that the government be shown to have taken the claimant's private property. The text of the Clause, which appears to make the existence of "private property" a necessary condition, suggests as much. And the Supreme Court has so held, in both traditional eminent domain and regulatory takings contexts.[87]

---

87. *See* United States v. Willow River Power Co., 324 U.S. 499, 511 (1945) (holding that claimant in eminent domain proceeding was not entitled to compensation for interest that was

Whether the government has taken "private property" is the least litigated of the four doctrinal requirements that flow from the language of the Takings Clause. The reason is not hard to find. Nearly all eminent domain actions seek to acquire interests that everyone concedes to be private property, such as a fee simple in land or an affirmative easement, such as a right-of-way.[88] And most regulatory takings cases arise in the context of disputes over land-use regulations. Here too, the claimant usually owns a fee simple (or perhaps a long-term lease) and alleges that the regulation has had the effect of taking all or part of this interest. So no issue arises about whether the private property element has been satisfied.

Occasionally, however, the Takings Clause is invoked in more unusual contexts, requiring courts to determine whether or not the government has taken an interest that qualifies as private property. Thus, the Court over the years has held that flowage easements, leases, trade secrets, security interests, and interest earned on deposits of money are private property for purposes of Takings Clause.[89]

not private property); Phillips v. Washington Legal Found., 524 U.S. 156, 172 (1998) (finding that interest on fund held by lawyer for clients was private property, and remanding for determination whether a regulation that transferred the interest to a third party was a taking).

88. One sample of appellate opinions finds that the power of eminent domain is used 99% of the time to acquire interests in land. Thomas W. Merrill, *The Economics of Public Use*, 72 CORNELL L. REV. 61, 95–96 (1986).

89. United States v. Virginia Elec. & Power Co., 365 U.S. 624, 631 (1961) (flowage easement); United States v. General

Conversely, it has determined that the head of water in rivers, delegated powers of eminent domain, future social security benefits, prospective business customers, and freedom from the imposition of general liabilities are not private property protected by the Clause.[90]

Although the question does not arise that often, the meaning of private property is arguably the most important determinant of the scope of the Takings Clause. The basic issue can be described in terms of the familiar metaphor of property as a "bundle of rights." If the Takings Clause applies only when a claimant loses certain standardized bundles of rights—such as fee simple ownership of land, affirmative easements, tangible personal property, and intellectual property rights—then the Clause is broad but not coextensive with all economic regulation. It is implicated only if the government takes without just compensation a fee simple in land, an easement, tangible personal property, or an intellectual property right.

Motors Corp., 323 U.S. 373, 381–83 (1945) (lease); Ruckelshaus v. Monsanto Co., 467 U.S. 986, 1003–04 (1984) (trade secrets); United States v. Security Indus. Bank, 459 U.S. 70, 75–76 (1982) (security interest); *Phillips*, 524 U.S. at 159 (interest on fund).

90. *Willow River*, 324 U.S. at 511 (head of water); United States *ex rel.* Tennessee Valley Auth. v. Powelson, 319 U.S. 266, 276–81 (1943) (delegated power of eminent domain); Flemming v. Nestor, 363 U.S. 603, 608 (1960) (future social security benefits); College Sav. Bank v. Florida Prepaid Postsecondary Educ. Expense Bd., 527 U.S. 666, 672 (1999) (prospective customers); Eastern Enter. v. Apfel, 524 U.S. 498, 539–40 (1998) (Kennedy, J., concurring in part and dissenting in part); *id.* at 554 (Breyer, J., dissenting) (1998) (immunity from liabilities).

If, in contrast, the Takings Clause applies whenever the claimant loses any individual "stick" or incident of property in the bundle of rights, then the domain of the Takings Clause is much larger. For example, if the right to transmit property upon death and the right to sell property are themselves deemed to be private property, then the Clause has a much more expansive domain.[91] It would be triggered by any regulation claimed to "take" the right to transmit or sell. In the limit, if every incident of property is itself private property, then the Takings Clause would be triggered by any governmental regulation that alters the distribution of wealth.[92]

Our view is that the conception of private property as standardized bundles of rights is more congruent both with the ordinary understanding of the constitutional language and with longstanding traditions associated with the Takings Clause—but the question is by no means settled.

A. The Dilemmas of Positivism

We begin with a background question: What is the source of law to which courts should look in determining whether or not an interest is private

91. *Cf.* Hodel v. Irving, 481 U.S. 704, 717 (1987) (holding that complete abrogation of right to inherit land is a taking); Andrus v. Allard, 444 U.S. 51, 67–68 (1979) (holding that abrogation of the right to sell eagle feathers is not a taking).

92. *See* Leif Wenar, *The Concept of Property and the Takings Clause*, 97 COLUM. L. REV. 1923, 1928 (1997).

property? The Supreme Court has offered the following important dictum on this topic:

> Property interests, of course, are not created by the Constitution. Rather they are created and their dimensions are defined by existing rules or understandings that stem from an independent source such as state law—rules or understandings that secure certain benefits and that support claims of entitlement to those benefits.[93]

This passage tells us a number of things. It tells us that private property is not itself a right created by the Constitution (the way the right of free speech, or more relevantly, the right to compensation for the taking of private property is). It tells us that property rights are identified and their dimensions are to be determined by consulting established provisions of positive law, meaning, in this context, nonconstitutional law. And it suggests that state law is an especially important component of the positive law that defines property.

But there is an important and unresolved ambiguity in the passage. The Court's endorsement of positive law as the source of private property could mean that we look to positive law both for the definition of private property and to determine whether any private property, as defined, has been

93. The passage is from Board of Regents v. Roth, 408 U.S. 564, 577 (1972), a leading procedural due process decision. But it has been quoted with approval in a number of takings cases. *See, e.g., Phillips*, 524 U.S. at 164; *Ruckelshaus*, 467 U.S. at 1001; Webb's Fabulous Pharmacies v. Beckwith, 449 U.S. 155, 161 (1980).

created. This we may call the "pure positivism" interpretation of the dictum. Alternatively, it could mean that courts must adopt a federal constitutional definition of private property, and then, armed with this definition, look to positive law to determine whether any private property, as defined, has been created. This we can call the "patterning definition" interpretation of the passage.[94] Although the Court has never resolved which interpretation is correct, several considerations suggest that pure positivism is problematic, and that the patterning definition approach is the better way to proceed in identifying private property.

One problem with pure positivism is that ceding control over the definition of private property to state courts and legislatures for federal constitutional law purposes could easily result in either too little or too much property, relative to common expectations about the meaning of property. For example, a state legislature could enact a law stating that after a certain date in the future, any person who purchases land shall have the right to exclude others, to use, and to dispose of the land, but such an interest "shall not be deemed to be private property." Although it is possible that the very enactment of such a statute would give rise to a takings claim by current owners, under pure positivism, those who acquire property after the statute takes effect would have no protection against takings. "A State would be allowed, in ef-

---

94. For further discussion of the distinction between these approaches, *see* Thomas W. Merrill, *The Landscape of Constitutional Property*, 86 VA. L. REV. 885, 949–54 (2000).

fect, to put an expiration date on the Takings Clause."[95]

The opposite problem could also emerge. States could adopt laws declaring that certain incidents of ownership valued by powerful interest groups are private property, in an effort to provide insurance against any future effort by legislatures or courts to change them. For example, a State in which the timber industry is powerful could declare that the privilege to clear cut forests is "private property," compelling the federal government to pay compensation to timber companies for any future federal regulations that impose limits on such practices.

More subtle problems would also arise. Suppose a State provides that owners of land subject to a development moratorium are to be issued transferable development rights (TDRs) that can be used or exchanged to permit development on other parcels of land.[96] Under pure positivism, one could argue that private property under state law includes the understanding that one gets nothing more than TDRs when development is denied. Thus, an attempt to seek greater compensation under the Takings Clause would automatically be denied, since this would presuppose that the claimant has more property than in fact is recognized by state law.[97]

95. Palazzolo v. Rhode Island, 533 U.S. 606, 608 (2001).

96. *See, e.g.,* Suitum v. Tahoe Reg'l Planning Agency, 520 U.S. 725 (1997); Penn Cent. Transp. Co. v. City of New York, 438 U.S. 104 (1978). TDRs are discussed further *infra* Chapters V(B)(2) and XI(C).

97. Those familiar with procedural due process law will recognize that this is a variation on the "bitter with the sweet" idea

In addition to these somewhat hypothetical problems, the outcomes of the Supreme Court's decisions are inconsistent with pure positivism. Consider *Keystone Bituminous Coal Ass'n v. De-Benedictis*.[98] The question was whether the State committed a taking when it abrogated an express waiver of surface support rights against the danger of subsidence from underground coal mining. Although Pennsylvania law expressly recognized that such waivers—a type of covenant running with the land—to be a separate "estate in land," the Court treated the support right as only an incident of property. In other words, the Court ignored the definition of private property found in state law and implicitly adopted its own definition, suggesting an unwillingness to abide by pure positivism.

Similarly, in *Palazzolo v. Rhode Island*,[99] the Court rejected the proposition that the content of an owner's bundle of rights is always qualified by development restrictions imposed by state law before the property was acquired. If the definition of private property were purely a matter of positive state law, it is difficult to see why the bundle of rights would not expand and contract as state law restrictions expand and contract. The Court's rejection of this idea presupposes that property has some

associated with the plurality opinion in Arnett v. Kennedy, 416 U.S. 134, 153–54 (1974), rejected in Cleveland Bd. of Educ. v. Loudermill, 470 U.S. 532, 540–41 (1985).

98.   480 U.S. 470 (1987).

99.   533 U.S. 606 (2001).

meaning independent of the collection of rules under state law about how resources may be used.

Particularly striking are two decisions that consider whether the right to earn interest on a sum of money is private property for purposes of the Takings Clause.[100] In both cases, state law provided quite clearly that interest earned on a particular type of deposit would be paid to someone other than the owner of the deposit. Thus, anyone who consulted "independent sources such as state law" prior to making a deposit should have known that they would receive no interest. Nevertheless, on both occasions, the Court held that the interest was the private property of the owner of the deposit, suggesting again that the Court is not prepared to accept the implications of pure positivism in defining private property.

The alternative approach—the patterning definition conception—avoids most of these pitfalls. If the definition of property is fixed as a matter of federal constitutional law, then the state cannot contract or expand the concept of property by *ipse dixit*. The state can create new interests—such as the condominium—that may qualify as property under the federal definition. Or it can abolish interests—such as dower and curtesy rights—that may qualify as property under the federal definition. The determination of what interests have been created at any given point in time would remain a matter of positive state law. But the characterization of those

100. *Phillips*, 524 U.S. at 159–60; *Webb's Fabulous Pharmacies*, 449 U.S. at 164–65.

interests as being either private property or something else would be a federal constitutional question, not a state law question.

The major drawback of the patterning definition approach is that it requires the Supreme Court to develop a federal constitutional definition of private property. Until very recently, the Court has been loath to embark on such an enterprise. In part, this reflects the influence of Legal Realism, which favored the open-ended "bundle of rights" conception of property, with the suggestion that the dimensions of property are always contingent and mutating.[101] If property is a purely contingent category of interests with no fixed meaning, then it would be foolish to attempt to formulate an abstract definition of private property for use in constitutional controversies.

But there is reason to believe that the Realist vision of property as a purely contingent bundle of rights is overdone. Certainly, in everyday life, people have no trouble identifying their own property as distinct from other people's property. As Bruce Ackerman has observed, "[m]ost of the time Layman negotiates his way through the complex web of property relationships that structures his social universe without even perceiving a need for expert guidance."[102] A concept that is applied by so many

101. *See* Thomas C. Grey, *The Disintegration of Property, in* PROPERTY: NOMOS XXII 69 (J. Roland Pennock & John W. Chapman eds., 1980).

102. BRUCE ACKERMAN, PRIVATE PROPERTY AND THE CONSTITUTION 116 (1977).

people in so many contexts in an unproblematic fashion must have some content about which it is possible to make meaningful generalizations. If this is so, then the prospect of developing a patterning definition of private property in order to ascertain what rights have been created as a matter of positive law need not seem so daunting.

B. Toward a Constitutional Definition of Property

The Supreme Court in recent years has in fact taken important steps toward developing a federal constitutional definition of private property. These steps are tentative, and arguably do not spell out a complete definition. We will begin by describing two elements of a federal definition that are implicitly supported by the general run of decided cases and explicitly recognized by recent Supreme Court decisions. We will then describe a third possible element that is more speculative, and does not enjoy any specific recognition from the Court.

1. Discrete Assets

The first element of a federal understanding of private property is that it refers to some right or set of rights that persons enjoy with respect to some discrete asset. In other words, private property refers to rights to some "thing," not to rights to bodily security, or personal privacy, or general shares of wealth, or a particular distribution of income.

This conclusion draws support from historical usage. The word "property" can of course refer general wealth, as in the sentence: "She is a woman of property." And occasionally "property" is used to refer to a broad range of rights.[103] But "private property" is rarely used in these senses; it most commonly refers to particular, owned things. Moreover, the phrase "nor shall private property be taken for public use" is not language one would most naturally adopt in order to prohibit governmental efforts to redistribute wealth or infringe on "inalienable" rights generally. Instead, this language, through the conjunction of the words "private property," "taken," and "for," conjures up the image of particular assets being acquired and redeployed to some public use.

Judges have also long understood, at least implicitly, that the Takings Clause protects particular things or assets, rather than fungible wealth. Courts have always assumed that general tax laws are not open to challenge under the Takings Clause.[104] Similarly, laws that impose fines or liabil-

103. In fact, James Madison wrote a famous essay shortly after the Bill of Rights was adopted in which he argued (perhaps metaphorically) that the term "property" should be understood to include personal rights, such as freedom of expression and religion. *See* James Madison, *Property*, PHIL. NAT'L GAZETTE, Mar. 27, 1792, *reprinted in* MIND OF THE FOUNDER: SOURCES ON THE POLITICAL THOUGHT OF JAMES MADISON 186–88 (Marvin Meyers ed., 1981).

104. *See* Penn Cent. Transp. Co. v. City of New York, 438 U.S. 104, 124 (1978); *see also* United States v. Sperry Corp., 493

ities payable out of general resources have been assumed to be immune from takings challenges. Although some scholars, most notably Richard Epstein, have argued that the Clause should apply to general shares of wealth,[105] this view has not caught on with the courts.

In a recent decision, five Justices expressly endorsed the understanding that private property refers to discrete resources. At issue in *Eastern Enterprises v. Apfel*[106] was a federal statute that retroactively increased the liability of employers in the coal mining industry to pay for health care benefits for retired employees. Although four Justices were prepared to strike down the statute under the Takings Clause,[107] five Justices objected that the Clause does not apply to a law that imposes only a general financial liability and does not affect identifiable assets.[108] In the view of the five who prevailed on this point, general financial liabilities do not interfere with any private property under the Takings Clause, and hence may be

U.S. 52, 59–60 (1989) (holding that a fee levied against an award from the Iran–United States Claims Tribunal does not constitute a taking). *See generally* JOHN LEWIS, A TREATISE ON THE LAW OF EMINENT DOMAIN 203–06 (1st ed. 1888); Eric Kades, *Drawing the Line Between Takings and Taxation: The Continuous Burdens Principle, and Its Broader Application* (forthcoming, Nw. U. L. REV.).

105. RICHARD A. EPSTEIN, TAKINGS: PRIVATE PROPERTY AND THE POWER OF EMINENT DOMAIN 93–104, 283–329 (1985).

106. Eastern Enters. v. Apfel, 524 U.S. 498 (1998).

107. *Id.* at 537.

108. *Id.* at 540 (Kennedy, J., concurring in part and dissenting in part); *id.* at 554 (Breyer, J., dissenting).

challenged only under the Due Process Clause. *Eastern Enterprises* thus confirms the longstanding view, previously reflected only in the pattern of holdings and the occasional dictum about taxes, that the Takings Clause is limited to private property in the form of discrete assets or "things."[109]

Does this limitation make sense? If we look only to the various rationales for compensation for takings surveyed in Chapter IIIB, it would seem not. If we view the Takings Clause as a type of mandatory insurance against government action that imposes disproportionate losses on particular persons, or as a mechanism for forcing the government to internalize the costs of its actions, or a means of neutralizing the unequal political influence of different groups, it seems silly to limit the Takings Clause to government action that affects discrete assets. Taxes or liability rules that single out one or a small number of persons for adverse treatment can present the same sorts of problems. The discrete asset limitation from this perspective arbitrarily cuts off the compensation requirement at a point that falls

109. Recent commentary by authors reflecting a variety of theoretical perspectives seeks to rehabilitate the idea that property entails rights to a "thing" and cannot be reduced to "bundle of rights" among persons. *See* J.E. PENNER, THE IDEA OF PROPERTY IN LAW (1997) (philosophical perspective); Craig Anthony Arnold, *The Reconstitution of Property: Property as a Web of Interests*, 26 HARV. ENV. L. REV. ___ (forthcoming, 2002) (environmental perspective); Thomas W. Merrill & Henry E. Smith, *What Happened to Property in Law and Economics?*, 111 YALE L.J. 357 (2001) (law-and-economics perspective).

well short of the underlying rationales for compensation.

Yet if we step back and recall that the Takings Clause is primarily designed to serve as a condition on the power of eminent domain—and on attempts by the government to evade that condition—the limitation to discrete assets does make sense. As discussed in Chapter IIIA, the power of eminent domain exists in order to permit the government to overcome problems of monopoly that arise when the government or its delegate needs to acquire unique resources to complete a particular project. These localized monopoly problems are caused by the private ownership of discrete assets, such as particular plots of land, or certain commodities in short supply, or critical intellectual property rights. The government has no need to condemn cash or other fungible assets. Thus, because the power in question—eminent domain—is limited to the acquisition of discrete assets, it makes sense that the constitutional limitation on that power—the Taking Clause's command that just compensation be paid for takings—should also be limited to discrete assets.

2. Right to Exclude

The second element of a general federal definition of private property is that it includes, as a necessary condition, authority generally to exclude others from a discrete asset.[110] The right to exclude has

110. We should perhaps add here that positive law must provide that the exclusion right is irrevocable for at least some

been recognized to be a defining feature of private property by a broad range of thinkers from Blackstone and Bentham to the present day. Certainly, what might be called core private property interests—possessory rights in real estate, tangible personal property, and intellectual property rights—are characterized by rights to exclude "all the world" from some thing. The person who is identified as the owner of the thing has the general power to exclude trespasses and other unwanted incursions by a large and indefinite class of others.[111] This feature is slightly harder to perceive with respect to nonpossessory property rights, such as future interests, easements, and water rights. Yet, even in these sorts of circumstances, the rights holder can call upon the state for protection against encroachments by other persons with an interest in the asset (present possessory owners, servient estates, and other riparians), or against third parties who seek to interfere with exercise of the nonpossessory right.

We also find that the Supreme Court's takings cases have given significant emphasis to this element of the definition. The Court has described the right to exclude as "one of the most essential"

period of time. *See* Merrill, *supra* note 94, at 978–79. Thus, a security guard can be given authority to exclude others from an asset, but this power is revocable and thus does not qualify as a property right.

111. On the importance of in rem rights of exclusion in defining property rights, *see* Thomas W. Merrill & Henry E. Smith, *The Property/Contract Interface*, 101 COLUM. L. REV. 773, 780–88 (2001).

rights of property, "one of the most treasured" rights, or something "universally held to be a fundamental element of the property right."[112] Although these statements have been made in the context of determining whether a particular regulation constitutes a taking, they confirm the perception that the right to exclude is central to the ordinary concept of private property.

More recently, the Court has given explicit recognition to the right to exclude as a necessary condition of finding that someone has a right of property. In *College Savings Bank v. Florida Prepaid Postsecondary Education Expense Board*,[113] the Court was faced with the question whether false advertising by a state agency violates the property rights of a private entity that provides a service in competition with the State. Noting that "[t]he hallmark of a protected property interest is the right to exclude others,"[114] the Court concluded that the state-sponsored false advertising did not implicate any property right, because the aggrieved private entity had no right to exclude others from the potential customers allegedly lured away by the State. Nor could the private party claim any property right in the activity of doing business or making a profit, since these were not assets from which the private party had the right to exclude others. Significantly, the Court made no effort to trace the importance of the right

112. *See* Kaiser Aetna v. United States, 444 U.S. 164, 176, 179–80 (1979); Loretto v. Teleprompter Manhattan CATV Corp., 458 U.S. 419, 435 (1982).

113. 527 U.S. 666 (1999).

114. *Id.* at 673.

to exclude to state law. The centrality of the exclusion right was asserted as a matter of direct federal constitutional interpretation.

By emphasizing the importance of the right to exclude in identifying private property, we do not read the Court as suggesting that every abrogation of the right to exclude is automatically a taking of property. Property exists when a person or entity has the right to exclude an open-ended set of others ("the world," or more accurately, "nearly all the world") from a discrete asset. As long as the person or entity retains a general right to exclude others, the fact that the state has abrogated the exclusion right in certain defined circumstances does not negate the existence of property. Thus, for example, the fact that an owner of land cannot exclude trespassers in circumstances of dire necessity,[115] or cannot exclude public aid workers seeking to visit migrant workers,[116] does not mean that the owner no longer has property, as long as the owner still has the generalized right to act as the gatekeeper of the asset. Abrogations of the right to exclude in particular circumstances can be challenged as takings, but such a challenge should be assessed under the categorical rules and *ad hoc* review standard for identifying regulatory takings discussed in Chapters V and VI; every abrogation of the right to exclude is not automatically a taking of property.[117]

115. Ploof v. Putnam, 71 A. 188 (Vt.1908).

116. State v. Shack, 277 A.2d 369 (N.J.1971).

117. For example, in PruneYard Shopping Ctr. v. Robins, 447 U.S. 74, 82–85 (1980), the Court applied the *ad hoc* review

3. *Exchangeable on a Stand–Alone Basis*

It is possible that the Supreme Court will not venture much beyond the right to exclude others from discrete assets as a rough federal definition of private property. But there are reasons to think that such a definition is incomplete—and overly broad. In particular, this bare-bones definition does not get us very far in solving the problem with which we began this chapter: Does private property refer only to pre-packaged bundles of rights, or is every stick and strand within the bundle itself private property? Consider several potential issues: (1) If property in land is burdened by covenants that run with the land, is each covenant itself private property? Or is a covenant just an incident of property, with the relevant unit of property being the land itself? (2) Owners of property are commonly recognized to have certain powers, such as the power to alienate, to transmit upon death, and to pledge the property as collateral for a loan. Are each of these powers themselves private property? Or is each just an incident of property? (3) Property in

standard and concluded that abrogration of the right to exclude political demonstrators from a shopping center to which the general public was invited was not a taking. In Loretto v. Teleprompter Manhattan CATV Corp., 458 U.S. 419 (1982), the Court held that a government order that permanently deprives the owner of an apartment of the right to exclude a cable television transmission line from the roof of the building was a categorical taking. In neither case, however, did the Court suggest that abrogation of the right to exclude in particular circumstances automatically nullifies the property rights of the owner of property.

land can often be subdivided into different physical strata, such as air rights, surface rights, and mineral rights. Are each of these strata themselves private property? Or are they just incidents of property?

One way to answer these sorts of questions would be to add an additional element to the federal definition of private property, to the effect that private property must be an interest that is exchangeable on a stand-alone basis. By exchangeable, we mean that the property can be exchanged in some fashion—bought, sold, pledged, or inherited. The exchange must be legal, in the sense that it is authorized by positive law. And it must not be purely hypothetical—exchange of similar assets must actually occur. By stand-alone basis, we mean that private property is something that is exchanged on a free-standing basis, without being bundled together with any other asset. Thus, rights, powers, and physical segments of assets that are exchanged only when bundled together with some other right, power or physical segment, would not be regarded as private property, at least not for takings purposes.

Although there is little explicit authority for such a requirement, there are several things to be said in support of it. First, limiting private property to assets exchangeable on a stand-alone basis is consistent with the history of the Takings Clause and the development of the regulatory takings doctrine. As we have seen, the Takings Clause was originally designed to function as a limitation on the power of eminent domain—a process by which the government acquires assets through forced exchange when it concludes that it would be too difficult or expensive to use voluntary exchange. This means that eminent domain is nearly always used to acquire assets that could be, and often are, exchangeable on a stand-alone basis. The regulatory takings doctrine, in turn, was developed to prevent the government from evading the constitutional limits on the power of eminent domain. The paradigmatic type of evasion is where the government uses its regulatory powers to acquire an asset that it should have acquired by eminent domain. Again, this means an asset that is exchangeable on a stand-alone basis. In short, defining private property to mean assets exchangeable on a stand-alone basis helps confine the Takings Clause and the regulatory takings doctrine to their conventional domains.

There is, in addition, a practical justification for limiting private property to interests that are exchangeable on a stand-alone basis. The remedy for a taking of private property is the award of monetary compensation, which is usually fixed by determining the fair market value of the interest taken.[118] Obviously, it will be much easier to determine the fair market value of an asset that is exchangeable on a stand-alone basis than it will be to try to determine the value of an interest or attribute that is only exchanged when bundled together with some other asset.

118. *See infra* Chapter VII.

Finally, the requirement that private property be exchangeable on a stand-alone basis appears to be consistent with most of outcomes courts have reached in takings controversies. As Saul Levmore has observed, as a predictive matter, the scope of the compensation requirement can be reliably determined by asking "whether a private party, with the same aims and strategy as the government ... would have needed to purchase property."[119] Thus, we find that those interests clearly regarded as private property—fee simple ownership of land and personal property, leases, affirmative easements, and intellectual property rights like patents and copyrights—all are exchangeable on a stand-alone basis. On the other hand, powers of property owners like the power to develop property or to transmit it upon death are not themselves exchangeable independently of the underlying asset. Significantly, these sorts of incidents are usually not regarded as private property for takings purposes.[120]

Even some of the more puzzling lines that have been drawn by the courts may be explainable on this basis. Consider the different treatment that has

119. Saul Levmore, *Takings, Torts, and Special Interests*, 77 VA. L. REV. 1333, 1340 (1991).

120. Admittedly, the Court has on occasion suggested that these sorts of incidents are fundamental to private property ownership. *See, e.g.*, Lucas v. South Carolina Coastal Council, 505 U.S. 1003, 1017–19 (1992) (suggesting that the right to develop land is a fundamental incident or attribute of ownership); Hodel v. Irving, 481 U.S. 704, 716 (1987) (suggesting that the right to inherit property is a core incident of ownership). In neither case, however, did the Court hold that these incidents were themselves private property.

been accorded to air rights and mineral rights. Mineral rights, which are often bought and sold independently of surface rights, generally receive full protection under the Takings Clause.[121] But courts have been much more reluctant to afford takings protection to air rights, which in fact are generally exchanged only together with rights to use and enjoy the surface area.[122] Or consider the different treatment of easements and covenants running with the land. Affirmative easements, such as rights of way, are often granted or acquired independently of the exchange of possessory interests in land. And we find that the Court has held that regulations imposing obligations that are tantamount to an affirmative easement are compensable takings.[123] Covenants restricting land, however, run to successors in interest only if there is some other grantor-grantee relationship between the originating parties; hence, running covenants are typically exchanged only when bundled together with some other asset, such as fee simple ownership

121. *See, e.g.*, Swanson v. Babbitt, 3 F.3d 1348, 1353 (9th Cir.1993) (noting that "[f]ederal mining claims are 'private property' which enjoy the full protection of the Fifth Amendment").

122. *See* Penn Cent. Transp. Co. v. City of New York, 438 U.S. 104, 135–38 (1978); *cf.* United States v. Causby, 328 U.S. 256, 266–67 (1946) (recognizing takings claim for airplane overflights when there was damage to use and enjoyment of surface rights).

123. *See Kaiser Aetna*, 444 U.S. at 178 (holding that regulation imposing public easement on marina was a taking); *Loretto*, 458 U.S. at 438 (holding that regulation requiring apartment building owner to permit cable television company to install permanent cable on rooftop was a taking).

of land or a lease of land. Decisions like *Keystone Bituminous Coal* suggest that the Court is reluctant to recognize covenants running with the land as private property rights for takings purposes.

Of course, there will always be problematic cases at the margins. The Court's decisions holding that interest earned on deposits of money is private property for takings purposes would appear to fall into this category.[124] We would guess that neither the interest earned on an interpleader fund nor the interest earned on a deposit placed with an attorney is, as a matter of current commercial practice, exchangeable on a stand-alone basis. But we are not completely sure about this. Interest payments today are often bundled together as "securitized" assets, and bought and sold in a secondary market.[125] So it is possible that interest earned on funds could qualify as something that is exchangeable on a stand-alone basis—or that it could satisfy this requirement at some point in the future.

C. The Problem of Conceptual Severance

The definition of private property has an important bearing on scope of the Takings Clause because

124. *See Phillips*, 524 U.S. at 159–60 (holding interest on money deposited by client with attorney is private property); *Webb's Fabulous Pharmacies*, 449 U.S. at 164–65 (holding interest earned on interpleader fund deposited with court is private property).

125. *See* Claire A. Hill, *Securitization: A Low–Cost Sweetener for Lemons*, 74 WASH. U. L.Q. 1061, 1068 (1996).

of what has been called the problem of "conceptual severance."[126] Under the bundle of rights metaphor, property can be physically subdivided into different horizontal and vertical segments, and it can be conceptually subdivided into different functional components. If each of these sticks or strands is itself private property, then every time the government regulates in such a way as to eliminate one of these fractional interests or functional components, it has committed a taking requiring just compensation. The Court has, in fact, recognized this danger, and has warned that "a claimant's parcel of property could not first be divided into what was taken and what was left for the purpose of demonstrating the taking of the former to be complete and hence compensable."[127] What the Court has not perceived is that the solution to the problem of conceptual severance lies—at least in significant part—in developing a satisfactory definition of private property.

In particular, if we reserve the status "private property" for certain standardized bundles of rights, as opposed to elevating every stick or strand in the bundle to the status of property, then the problem of conceptual severance is greatly reduced.

126. Margaret Jane Radin, *The Liberal Conception of Property: Cross Currents in the Jurisprudence of Takings*, 88 COLUM. L. REV. 1667, 1677 (1988).

127. Concrete Pipe & Prods., Inc. v. Construction Laborers Pension Trust for S. Cal., 508 U.S. 602, 644 (1993). *See also* Tahoe–Sierra Preservation Council, Inc. v. Tahoe Regional Planning Agency, 122 S.Ct. 1465, 1483 (2002) ("Of course, defining the property interest taken in terms of the very regulation being challenged is circular.").

The three-part definition canvassed in the last section would have this effect. It would limit the protection of the Takings Clause to conventional private property interests—pre-packaged bundles in which persons have the right to exclude others from discrete assets that are exchangeable on a stand-alone basis. The Takings Clause would come into play when the government is alleged to have taken a fee simple in land, a lease, an affirmative easement, tangible personal property, or intellectual property. But it would not be triggered by a contention that the government has taken a particular incident of property, such as the right to inherit or sell, or has taken a covenant that runs with the land.

Clarifying the definition of property in this fashion would also resolve other apparent anomalies in takings law. It would explain why condemnation of a very small amount of land—for a street widening for example—is always regarded as a taking, whereas the imposition of a large building setback requirement usually is not.[128] In the former case, the government has taken an exchangeable interest in private property—a narrow fee simple in land—whereas, in the latter case, the government has imposed a restriction on the use of land, which restriction can be imposed as a covenant running with the land, but is not ordinarily exchangeable on a stand-alone basis. The use restriction could be challenged as a taking, but only on the ground that

128. *See, e.g.,* Gorieb v. Fox, 274 U.S. 603, 610 (1927) (upholding setback ordinance against takings challenge).

it has such a severe impact on the value of the underlying fee that it is the functional equivalent of the taking of private property in the form of a fee simple.

A better definition of private property also goes a long way toward solving the numerator-denominator problem in determining the extent of diminution in value in regulatory takings cases (considered further in Chapters V and VI). To calculate diminution in value, one must compare what has been lost due to regulation (the numerator) with what the claimant had before the regulation was imposed (the denominator). Understanding the definition of private property tells us that the denominator can never be an interest smaller than a recognized interest in private property. Thus, if we conclude that air rights do not qualify as private property, because typically they are not exchangeable on a stand-alone basis, then the denominator in the *Penn Central* case could not be the value of the air rights themselves. The denominator would have to be the larger fee simple in the parcel as a whole, as the Court held.[129]

Clarifying the definition of private property in this fashion does not solve all dilemmas about numerators and denominators. When an owner holds title to several parcels of land that are contiguous or located in close proximity, it is still necessary to determine whether the denominator is a single lot, or several contiguous lots, or all land owned by the

129. *Penn Cent.*, 438 U.S. at 130–31.

same individual in the vicinity.[130] Since each lot constitutes private property, the definition of private property cannot help us in figuring out the answer to this puzzle. But resolving the definition of private property should put an end to many numerator-denominator problems based on vertical segmentation of land or functional severance of interests in property. This by itself would be a significant contribution.

130. *See* John E. Fee, Comment, *Unearthing the Denominator in Regulatory Takings Claims*, 61 U. CHI. L. REV. 1535, 1535–37 (1994).

CHAPTER V

TAKINGS: CATEGORICAL RULES

Once the private property threshold is satisfied, the next step is to ask whether this interest has been "taken" by the government. In ordinary usage, to "take" property means to acquire "possession or control" of it.[131] This most likely was also the original understanding of the term. As we saw in Chapter II, in the colonial era, compensation was generally paid when government appropriated or destroyed private property, but not when it reduced the value of property through regulation. Those who ratified the Fifth Amendment thus most probably understood "taking" to refer to government action that transfers possession of private property from citizen to state, or that has the same effect as depriving the owner of possession.

If the Takings Clause were limited to exercises of the power of eminent domain, there would never be any debate about whether there has been a "taking." Eminent domain results in the formal transfer of title from the citizen to the state, and hence, there will never be any doubt that the government has assumed "possession or control" of the property. But the Clause by its terms is not limited to eminent domain, and the Court has not construed it

131. WEBSTER'S NEW INTERNATIONAL DICTIONARY (2d ed. 1954).

as being so limited. In the pivotal decision of *Pennsylvania Coal Co. v. Mahon*,[132] the Court ruled that the government cannot use the police power to achieve a result that should have been accomplished using the power of eminent domain. This means, at a minimum, that exercises of the police power having an effect that is the functional equivalent of a taking of private property for public use must also be accompanied by the payment of just compensation. *Pennsylvania Coal* gave rise to the understanding that some police power regulations have such a serious impact on property rights that they must be regarded as a taking, that is, it gave rise to the regulatory takings doctrine.

In deciding whether challenged government action constitutes a taking, the Supreme Court in recent years has employed a bifurcated inquiry. The first level, which we call categorical review, considers whether the action falls within some category for which compensation is *always* required as a matter of constitutional law, or some category for which compensation is *never* required. The idea behind this categorical approach is that there are certain government actions that either so clearly demand compensation or are so clearly immune from liability for compensation that they require no case-specific judgment by courts. The second level of review, which we call *ad hoc* review, occurs only if

132. 260 U.S. 393 (1922). Before *Mahon*, the courts had sent mixed messages, sometimes limiting the Takings Clause to appropriations, and sometimes suggesting it might have a broader application. *See* Kris W. Kobach, *The Origins of Regulatory Takings: Setting the Record Straight*, 1996 UTAH L. REV. 1211.

the categorical tests for compensation or no compensation do not apply. This second-level review is explicitly open-ended, entailing a case-by-case balancing of rather poorly defined factors.

Most of the activity in recent years has concerned categorical review. The Supreme Court has expanded the categories of actions that are *per se* or automatic takings, and arguably has narrowed the categories of actions that *per se* or automatically do not require compensation.[133] This Chapter explores the rationale and scope of categorical review; the next Chapter takes up *ad hoc* review.

A. The Rationale for Categorical Takings Rules

The use of categorical rules to identify takings can be explained both in terms of the history of the regulatory takings doctrine and with reference to the theories that have been advanced in support of

133. The Court's two most recent decisions, however, run counter to this trend. In Palazzolo v. Rhode Island, 533 U.S. 606 (2001), the Court rejected a *per se* rule of nonliability for regulatory restrictions in effect at the time the owner acquires title, ruling that any reduced expectation caused by such a restriction should be assessed under the *ad hoc* standard. And in Tahoe–Sierra Preservation Council, Inc. v. Tahoe Regional Planning Agency, 122 S.Ct. 1465 (2002), the Court rejected a categorical rule of liability for development moratoria that temporarily eliminate all economically beneficial use of land, again instructing that such a restriction should be assessed under the *ad hoc* approach. It is too early to tell if these decisions portend a more general shift away from categorical rules in favor of the *ad hoc* method.

compensating property owners for some types of losses associated with government action.

From an historical perspective, categorical rules can be seen as emerging from a prolonged effort by courts to locate the ill-defined boundary between the power of eminent domain and the police power. *Pennsylvania Coal* depicts these powers as blending into each other by imperceptible degrees.[134] If that is the case, then one way of deciding whether particular actions fall on one side of the line or the other is to start by identifying paradigm cases at either end of the spectrum. Courts can then reason by analogy from these paradigm cases to identify other types of action that are sufficiently similar that they warrant similar treatment. Over time, this produces a cluster of situations near both ends of the spectrum that can be resolved by categorical rules without any detailed analysis of the individual factors they present. This leaves only the gray area in the middle where actions must be judged individually to determine the side of the line on which they fall.

It is not hard to see evidence of this kind of process at work in the history of regulatory takings law. The paradigm case of eminent domain authority is the formal condemnation of property by the government, resulting in a transfer of all rights of possession, use and enjoyment associated with the property to the government or its designee. A good

---

134. *Pennsylvania Coal*, 260 U.S. at 416 ("As we have already said, this is a question of degree—and therefore cannot be disposed of by general propositions.")

example of reasoning from this paradigm is *Pumpelly v. Green Bay Co.*,[135] an early case in which the government had approved the construction of a dam that permanently flooded the plaintiff's property. Although there was no formal exercise of eminent domain and no transfer of title to the government, the Court reasoned that the flooding deprived the owner of all use and enjoyment of the property in a manner similar to a condemnation, and hence, the action should have proceeded under the power of eminent domain.[136]

The paradigm case of the police power is a regulation designed to prevent a public nuisance. An example of reasoning from the public nuisance paradigm is *Village of Euclid v. Ambler Realty Co.*,[137] in which a suburb of Cleveland, Ohio adopted a comprehensive zoning ordinance that placed all undeveloped land into different zones of permitted uses. Although there was no showing that the more restricted uses would inevitably create a nuisance subject to abatement at common law, the Court sustained the scheme on the ground that it was

135. Pumpelly v. Green Bay Co., 80 U.S. 166 (1872).

136. The Court's recent decision in *Tahoe–Sierra* exemplifies the centrality of paradigm cases in regulatory takings jurisprudence: Both the majority opinion and the principal dissenting opinion argue by way of analogy to the paradigm case of eminent domain in addressing the claim that a development moratorium constitutes a *per se* taking. The majority emphasizes that such a moratorium is not like eminent domain because the government does not acquire possession of the property. The dissent emphasizes that such a moratorium is like eminent domain, because it is functionally similar to condemnation of a leasehold estate.

137. 272 U.S. 365 (1926).

designed to minimize the incidence of future nuisances, and hence was a legitimate exercise of the police power and did not require any payment of compensation.

The modern Court's categorical rules can be seen as a natural outgrowth of this process of reasoning by analogy from uncontested paradigms. After a sufficient number of precedents accumulate, the Court identifies certain clusters of outcomes and seeks to generalize their features and restate them as a rule. This evolutionary pattern is similar to what we see in other areas of law, such as antitrust, where general standards eventually crystallize into *per se* rules of liability (or nonliability) as courts respond to repeated exposure to certain patterns of conduct.

The use of categorical rules can also be explained in terms of the theories surveyed in Chapter III. One prominent theme of takings theory, reflected most prominently in Michelman's discussion of demoralization costs,[138] is the goal of reducing the risk associated with uncompensated losses. One source of risk is uncertainty about legal rules, and in particular, about whether certain types of government action will or will not require the payment of compensation. Categorical rules designed to produce consistent outcomes under readily identifiable states of fact can be seen as a strategy for reducing legal risk, and hence reducing demoralization costs.

138. *See* Frank I. Michelman, *Property, Utility, and Fairness: Comments on the Ethical Foundations of "Just Compensation,"* 80 HARV. L. REV. 1165, 1217 (1967).

Of course, categorical rules only reduce uncertainty if they are coherent and predictable in their application. This, as we shall see, is not obviously the case with respect to some of the categorical rules the Court has adopted.[139]

A second and more general theme of the discussion in Chapter III is the need to reduce the amount of information that must be gathered and processed by a court before it can decide whether compensation is required because of some government action. Michelman's theory, for example, requires a comparison of the demoralization costs associated with uncompensated government action and the settlement costs of identifying claimants and calculating and paying compensation to them.[140] Similarly, the fiscal illusion theory requires that we compare the benefits from requiring that the government internalize the costs of regulation with the benefits from requiring that property owners internalize the costs of engaging in activity subject to regulation.[141] In-

---

139. On the economic and other costs that may result from a lack of predictability as to when compensation is payable, *see* Lawrence Blume & Daniel Rubinfeld, *Compensation for Takings: An Economic Analysis*, 72 Cal. L. Rev. 569 (1989). Predictability can also have costs, however. For example, if landowners know that physical invasions by the government predictably trigger a full compensation requirement, they may make no efforts to minimize investments in areas in which the government likely will need to condemn property for some future public need, such as airport expansion. *See generally* Louis Kaplow, *An Economic Analysis of Legal Transitions*, 99 Harv. L. Rev. 509, 529–36 (1986).

140. *See supra* Chapter IIIB1.

141. *See supra* Chapter IIIB2.

formation about these kinds of variables—demoralization costs, settlement costs, government cost-internalization, private party cost-internalization—is not the sort of thing that litigants and courts ordinarily consider. This suggests that if the judiciary is to render decisions that make sense in terms of takings theory, they will have to make use of a more formalistic doctrine, *i.e.*, categorical rules, that reduces the amount of information that must be gathered and processed.

One question that needs to be asked in this connection is whether the Supreme Court is the right institution to develop categorical rules for determining when compensation must be paid. If compensation policy requires gathering and processing large amounts of information unfamiliar to courts, then perhaps some other institution (such as an administrative agency) would be better suited to the task. The only answer that can be given, however unsatisfactory, is that once we make compensation for takings a constitutional right, and once we implement that right through litigation, the court of final appeal in constitutional cases necessarily has the last word in formulating the relevant decisional rules. If it is necessary to develop categorical rules in order to implement a compensation requirement that makes sense from a policy perspective, then, for better or worse, those rules must be established and enforced by the Supreme Court.

B. Government Actions that are *Per se* Takings

The Court has recognized a number of situations that are *per se* or automatically regarded as takings. The most important, of course, is when the government formally exercises the power of eminent domain. No one questions that this is always regarded as a taking. Two other categorical rules—for permanent physical occupations and complete loss of economic value—have proven to be more controversial.

1. *Permanent Physical Occupation*

The Supreme Court has held that "permanent physical occupations" by the government constitute takings requiring the payment of compensation, no matter how trivial the economic impact of the occupation or how reasonable the government rationale for the occupation. The rule that permanent physical occupations are takings *per se* was developed most fully by the Court in *Loretto v. Teleprompter Manhattan CATV Corp.*,[142] and has been reaffirmed a number of times since then. The Court in *Loretto* held that a New York law requiring a landlord to permit a cable television company to install a cable over the roof and down the side of her building was a taking, notwithstanding the fact that the cable was installed by a third party (the cable company, not the government itself) and occupied only a trivial space on the building.

142.   458 U.S. 419, 435–38 (1982).

The Court drew on both history and policy analysis in support of this categorical rule. With respect to history, the Court concluded from a review of its prior cases that although government action that takes the form of a physical invasion of property is not always deemed to be a taking, "[w]hen faced with a constitutional challenge to a *permanent* physical occupation of real property, this Court has invariably found a taking."[143] Indeed, the feature of the New York law that probably made it most difficult to sustain was that it in effect compelled the transfer of an affirmative utility easement from the owner of the building to the cable company. Utility easements are exchangeable on a stand-alone basis and are ordinarily obtained through the exercise of eminent domain. Thus, to uphold the New York law would allow the government to do an end run about the Takings Clause by relabeling the condemnation of an easement as a police power regulation.

The Court also relied on policy analysis, noting that permanent physical occupations are an especially demoralizing form of government interference because "an owner suffers a special kind of injury when a stranger directly invades and occupies the owner's property."[144] Finally, the Court justified the application of a categorical rule for permanent occupations on the ground that this would avoid "otherwise difficult line-drawing problems" and would

143. *Id.* at 427 (emphasis added).

144. *Id.* at 436 (emphasis deleted).

present "relatively few problems of proof."[145] In other words, the rule would reduce the information-gathering and processing costs that would otherwise be incurred in examining this category of government action under the open-ended *ad hoc* test.

Although the Court made it sound plausible that permanent physical occupations mandated by the government could be readily identified as a special case, subsequent decisions have revealed that the rule rests on a number of problematic distinctions. The first is the distinction between a temporary and a permanent occupation. How long an occupation must continue—or be thought likely to continue—to qualify as "permanent" is nowhere defined in *Loretto* or subsequent opinions. For example, in a subsequent decision involving exactions of public easements of access from landowners, the Court suggested that repeated but non-continuous use of private property by the public is equivalent to a permanent physical occupation.[146] But one might just as easily conceptualize such recurring public access as a series of temporary physical invasions or occupations.

The second—and probably even more problematic—distinction is that between a government-mandated occupation of property by third parties (a categorical taking) and use regulations that functionally achieve the same result (not a categorical taking). In *Loretto*, the Court reasoned that the

145. *Id.* at 437.

146. *See* Nollan v. California Coastal Comm'n, 483 U.S. 825, 831 (1987).

categorical rule was applicable because the cable company owned the cable in question and hence the landlord suffered from a permanent physical intrusion. The implication is that New York could have avoided the categorical rule by requiring the landlord to purchase and install the cable herself. But since the physical impact of these two approaches on the landlord's property would have been identical, it is far from clear why the Court should treat them differently for takings clause purposes. Indeed, if anything, requiring that the landlord buy and install a cable arguably seems more onerous than requiring that she allow someone else to install a cable. Nevertheless, a majority of the Justices has continued to adhere to the view that there is something distinctively intrusive—"qualitatively more severe"[147]—about regulation that entails the mandated presence of an item or person unowned or unaffiliated with the landowner on the landowner's property.

A third problematic distinction is between "voluntary" or invited third-party presences and uninvited or involuntary third-party physical invasions or occupations. The Court has sometimes held that a third party's presence on private property that a landowner must accept in order to obtain government permission to engage in certain businesses is a permanent physical occupation subject to the categorical rule, and at other times has conceptualized such a third party's presence as merely "voluntary" and hence not subject to the rule. In *Loretto*, the

147. *Loretto*, 458 U.S. at 436.

Court conceded that the landlord could avoid the cable installation requirements by ceasing to rent the building to tenants, "[b]ut a landlord's ability to rent his property may not be conditioned on his forfeiting the right to compensation for a physical occupation...."[148] In subsequent cases, however, the Court held that the statutes at issue did not effect a government-mandated physical occupation because the landowners "voluntarily rented their land" and the regulatory scheme did not compel them to continue to do so.[149]

Still another question about the categorical rule for permanent physical occupations is whether it is limited to land, or might also apply to personal or even intellectual property. Would, for example, a requirement that a company allow public access to one of its websites constitute a categorical taking as a kind of mandated third-party occupation? At various points, the Court has noted that property interests in land deserve special protection, if only for reasons of history and tradition,[150] but it is unclear how far this privileging of rights in land goes.

148. *Id.* at 439 n.17.

149. *See* Yee v. City of Escondido, 503 U.S. 519, 527 (1992) (upholding rent control scheme against a takings challenge); FCC v. Florida Power Corp., 480 U.S. 245, 250–53 (1987) (holding that regulation of prices electric utilities charge cable companies for pole attachments is not subject to *Loretto* because the original relationship was voluntary).

150. Most prominently, Justice Scalia wrote in *Lucas*:

In the case of personal property, by reason of the State's traditionally high degree of control over commercial dealings, [the property owner] ought to be aware of the possibility that new regulation might even render his property economically

A final question concerning the permanent physical occupation rule is whether it is subject to any sort of nuisance exception. If, for example, the government permanently occupied land in order to monitor the risk of earthquakes, or to track an underground water pollution plume, would the government have to pay damages, or would the court regard the intrusion as falling within our general legal tradition that places implicit limits on property rights that harm the public?[151] For more on nuisance and takings, see below.

2. Complete Loss of Economic Value

The categorical rule for permanent physical occupations has nothing to do with economic impact; *Loretto,* a case in which the Court found a taking in the absence of any significant economic impact, could not be clearer on that point. By contrast, the second category of categorical takings—complete loss of economic value or total wipeout—has every-

worthless.... In the case of land, however, we think the notion ... that title is somehow held subject to the "implied limitation" that the State may subsequently eliminate all economically valuable use is inconsistent with the historical compact recorded in the Takings Clause that has become part of our constitutional culture.

Lucas, 505 U.S. at 1027–28.

151. At least one court has indicated that government occupation of property for purposes of monitoring contamination could constitute a taking. *See* Hendler v. United States, 952 F.2d 1364, 1375 (Fed.Cir.1991) (suggesting that EPA's requirement of access to a property bordering on a contaminated site in order to monitor the flow of groundwater pollution could constitute a taking under the permanent physical occupation rule).

thing to do with economic impact. These two categories, viewed together, thus illustrate the difficulty of reducing the Takings Clause either to a form of insurance against economic losses or to a prophylactic against unfair or oppressive government action.[152]

Complete loss of economic value is a variant of the "diminution in value" test which plays a large role in *ad hoc* takings analysis. The diminution in value test concerns how much a given government regulation has reduced the market value of some specific property. It is a (deceptively) precise test, in that it yields a specific, arithmetically derived answer for each case: One simply compares the value of the property after the regulation went into effect (the numerator) with its value before the regulation went into effect (the denominator). The categorical rule for complete loss of economic value appears to say that if the fraction equals zero—if the government regulation leaves the property without any market value—then, with the caveats discussed below, the government regulation automatically qualifies as a taking.

That at least is what the Supreme Court has said several times in dicta and what a bare majority held in *Lucas v. South Carolina Coastal Council*.[153] In *Lucas*, the landowner owned two beachfront lots that were subject to post-acquisition restrictions on development contained in the South Carolina Beachfront Management Act. The trial court held

152. For an extended treatment of this difficulty *see* Jeremy Paul, *The Hidden Structure of Takings Law*, 64 S. CAL. L. REV. 1393 (1991).

153. 505 U.S. 1003 (1992).

that the restrictions rendered the lots "valueless," and, despite objections from the dissenters that the factual record did not support this conclusion and that the Court was not required to adhere to it, Justice Scalia's majority opinion took the finding as given. The majority concluded that the restrictions warranted "categorical treatment" as takings because they entailed a situation in which regulation "denies all economically beneficial or productive use of land."[154]

The Court sought to justify its categorical rule by stressing the functional equivalence between regulations that deprive owners of all economic value and formal exercises of eminent domain. The Court suggested that the primary justification for the rule is that "total deprivation of beneficial use is, from the landowner's point of view, the equivalent of a physical appropriation."[155] Justice Scalia said that this was especially true where the regulation had the effect of barring any development of land. He observed: "[t]he many statutes on the books, both state and federal, that provide for the use of eminent domain to impose servitudes on private scenic lands preventing developmental uses, or to acquire such lands altogether, suggest the practical equivalence in this setting of negative regulation and appropriation."[156]

154. *Id.* at 1015.

155. *Id.* at 1017.

156. *Id.* at 1018–19. *Cf. id.* at 1066 (Stevens, J., dissenting) ("From the landowner's point of view, a regulation that dimin-

The Court also intimated more general theoretical reasons for subjecting complete losses in value to *per se* treatment. The Court suggested that government action that deprives an owner of all economic value without compensation suggests a failure of ordinary political processes. "[I]n the extraordinary circumstances when *no* productive or economically beneficial use of land is permitted, it is less realistic to indulge our usual assumption that the legislature is simply 'adjusting the benefits and burdens of economic life' in a manner that secures an 'average reciprocity of advantage' to everyone concerned."[157] On the contrary, the Court said, such regulations "carry with them a heightened risk that private property is being pressed into some form of public service under the guise of mitigating serious public harm."[158] In addition, the Court suggested that the failure to compensate for the loss of value associated with many regulations is a product of necessity, quoting Justice Holmes' statement in *Pennsylvania Coal* that "Government hardly could go on if to

ishes a lot's value by 50% is as well 'the equivalent' of the condemnation of half of the lot. Yet it is well established that a 50% diminution in value does not by itself constitute a taking.").

157. *Id.* at 1017–18 (citations omitted).

158. *Id.* at 1017. The parentheticals following this explanation suggest that Justice Scalia equates ecologically-oriented natural preservation with "public service" or public benefit, and more traditional human health and safety concerns with genuine public harm. Elsewhere in the opinion, however, Justice Scalia appeared to reject any reliance on the distinction between benefit creation and harm prevention, arguing that the distinction "is often in the eye of the beholder." *Id.* at 1024.

some extent values incident to property could not be diminished without paying for every such change in the general law."[159] But this concern with limiting settlement costs, the Court thought, has less force where regulations deprive owners of all economic value, because such regulations are "relatively rare."[160]

Like the permanent physical occupation rule, the rule that total economic wipeouts are categorically takings raises a number of interpretive problems in actual application. For one thing, it is not clear what it means to say a given property is valueless. In *Lucas*, even assuming the lots could not be built on, the landowner probably could have obtained some money for the property as buffer lots for neighbors who had built houses in the area before the building restrictions went into effect.[161] The majority ignored this possibility, raising the question whether it intended the categorical rule to apply only to true deprivations of all market value, or perhaps it assumed that the rule would be triggered by any regulation that prohibits all development of land. If the former is true, then the categorical test does not amount to much in practice, since it will rarely apply. But if the latter is true, then the categorical rule for total wipeouts has the potential to encompass a significant class of land-

159. *Id.* at 1018 (*quoting Pennsylvania Coal*, 260 U.S. at 413).

160. *Id.* at 1018.

161. *Id.* at 1044 (Blackmun, J., dissenting).

use regulations.[162]

The Court's recent decision in *Tahoe–Sierra Preservation Council v. Tahoe Regional Planning Agency*[163] contains language suggesting that *Lucas* adopts the former definition: A complete deprivation of economically beneficial use means that the property has zero market value. But the issue in *Tahoe–Sierra*—whether a temporary growth moratorium constitutes a *per se* taking—actually was quite limited, and hence much of the majority's language regarding *Lucas* could be regarded as dictum.[164] Interestingly, however, the three dissenters

162. The Court of Federal Claims in the *Florida Rock* litigation attempted to expand the total wipeout category in precisely this way. *See* Florida Rock Inds. v. United States, 21 Cl.Ct. 161 (1990), *vacated and remanded*, 18 F.3d 1560 (Fed.Cir.1994). The Court's more recent decision in *Palazzolo v. Rhode Island*, 533 U.S. 606, 631 (2001), holds that a regulation that permits the construction of at least one "substantial residence" on an 18–acre tract cannot be a total wipeout as a matter of law. This does not shed much light on the ambiguity about what "total wipeout" means, for the holding is consistent with either the zero market value or the no development interpretation.

163. 122 S.Ct. 1465 (2002).

164. Moreover, even if *Tahoe–Sierra* does stand for the broad proposition that any government regulation that is less than permanent triggers *Penn Central* rather than *Lucas* review, that proposition does not tell us what "permanent" means in the context of land use regulation. *See* 122 S.Ct. at 1492 (Rehnquist, C.J. dissenting) ("a distinction between 'temporary' and 'permanent' prohibitions is tenuous.... Land-use regulations are not irrevocable. And the government can even abandon condemned land.") The difficulty of differentiating meaningfully between "permanent" and "temporary" regulation also besets the Court's physical occupation case law, as discussed *supra* Chapter VB1.

(including Justice Scalia, the author of *Lucas*) made clear that they regard *Lucas* as adopting the latter definition: An owner has been deprived of all economically beneficial use whenever a regulation forbids any physical transformation of the land, even if such a ban leaves the land with some (albeit reduced) market value. It is thus unlikely that *Tahoe–Sierra* will be the last word on the subject.

Another major uncertainty regarding the total wipeout rule concerns how the unit of property is to be defined or delimited for purposes of application of the diminution of value test—the numerator/denominator problem alluded to at the end of Chapter IV.[165] If a claimant's property interest before the regulation is imposed (the denominator) can be broadly construed, then it may be easier for the government to identify some positive market value left over (the numerator) after application of the regulation. For example, if a landowner buys two adjoining lots with separate deeds in a single closing, and one lot is wetland and one upland, is the relevant property interest for Takings Clause purposes the two lots together or is it the wetland lot alone, assuming it becomes subject to development

165. We suggested there that paying closer attention to established categories of property would help limit the potential for conceptually severing property along functional lines. The numerator/denominator problem under the diminution in value test primarily concerns the physical dimensions of the property rather than its functional dimensions. Since property in land generally can be divided up or combined together into smaller or larger parcels without legal limitation, the solution to the numerator/denominator problem in this context probably cannot be found by refining the definition of property.

restrictions? And does the answer to that question change if the wetland and upland were held subject to a single deed? The lower court case law on the question of how to define the denominator for the purpose of the total diminution test is not instructive, and the Supreme Court has steadfastly refused to clarify matters. In *Lucas*, Justice Scalia acknowledged the problem: "regrettably, the rhetorical force of our 'deprivation of all economically feasible use' rule is greater than its precision, since the rule does not make clear the 'property interest' against which the loss of value is to be measured."[166] In *Tahoe–Sierra*, the Court again acknowledged the importance of defining the denominator and reiterated that the analysis must focus on a regulation's impact on "the parcel as a whole,"[167] but it failed to articulate any general principles for defining "the parcel."

The third—and perhaps most important—complexity with the total deprivation rule is that it is not really a categorical rule at all, because it is subject to a common-law nuisance exception. Before the Court's decision in *Lucas*, the case law seemed to indicate that a potentially broad "nuisance" exception exists to takings liability, even where regulations render a property interest valueless or near-

166. *Lucas*, 505 U.S. at 1016 n.7. More recently, in Palazzolo v. Rhode Island, 533 U.S. 606, 629 (2001), a case involving an 18–acre tract that contained both wetland and upland, the Court again refused to answer the question of how the denominator is to be defined, finding that the issue had not been preserved in the courts below.

167. *Tahoe–Sierra*, 122 S.Ct. at 1483–84.

ly so.[168] Justice Scalia's opinion in *Lucas* rejects a broad nuisance exception to takings liability, but nevertheless recognizes a limited, common law exception to liability. As he put it, the categorical rule does not apply where the regulation at issue merely reflects common law principles already in place before the acquisition of title:

> Any limitation so severe [as to deprive the owner of all economic value] cannot be newly legislated or decreed (without compensation), but must inhere in the title itself, in the restrictions that background principles of the State's law of property and nuisance already place upon land ownership. A law or decree with such an effect must, in other words, do no more than duplicate the result that could have been achieved in the courts—by adjacent landowners (or other uniquely affected persons) under the State's law of private nuisance, or by the State under its complementary power to abate nuisances that affect the public generally, or otherwise.[169]

It is extremely hard to say how this common law nuisance exception should be fleshed out.[170] One set

168. *See, e.g.*, Keystone Bituminous Coal Ass'n v. DeBenedictis, 480 U.S. 470, 491 (1987) (referring to "[t]he Court's hesitance to find a taking when the State merely restrains uses of property that are tantamount to public nuisances").

169. 505 U.S. at 1029.

170. *See* Lynn E. Blais, *Takings, Statutes, and the Common Law: Considering Inherent Limitations on Title*, 70 S. CAL. L. REV. 1, 2 (1996) (arguing that the uncertainty created by *Lucas* will be "enormous" and criticizing the decision for privileging

of questions concerns the source of law for defining the exception. Evidently only common law principles are relevant; statutes and regulations are to be ignored. Justice Kennedy concurred only in the judgment in *Lucas*, noting specifically his objection to defining the exception solely in terms of the common law,[171] and his interpretation of the majority opinion on this point went unchallenged. But it is unclear whether the common law of nuisance is to be determined in terms of the common law of the State in which the property is located, or to "general" common law principles, or to some federalized definition. (In this sense, the common law nuisance exception presents analytical difficulties similar to those that surround the definition of "private property," discussed in Chapter IV.) [172]

pre-existing common law, as opposed to statutes, as constitutionally significant limitations on title).

171. *Lucas*, 505 U.S. at 1035 (Kennedy, J., concurring in the judgment). This is reinforced by *Palazzolo*, where the Court declined to recognize any general exception for regulatory limitations imposed on property at the time the owner acquires title. *See* 533 U.S. at 629. In contrast, the dissenters in *Tahoe–Sierra*—who formed part of the majority in *Lucas* and *Palazzolo*—suggested that routine zoning statutes and regulations also constitute part of the background property principles pursuant to which acquirors of land take title. *See Tahoe–Sierra*, 122 S.Ct. at 1494–95 (Rehnquist, C.J., dissenting) ("Zoning regulations existed as far back as colonial Boston.... Thus, the short-term delays attendant to zoning and permit regimes are a longstanding feature of state property law and part of a landowner's reasonable investment-backed expectations.").

172. There are suggestions in Justice Scalia's opinion that the Restatement of Torts provides an appropriate guide to defining a common law nuisance. *Lucas*, 505 U.S. at 1031 (repeatedly citing RESTATEMENT (SECOND) OF TORTS). The uncertainty about the

Under any definition, the nuisance law of most States typically employs a broad reasonableness test that turns on an examination of the facts of each case. Ironically, this case-by-case inquiry would seem to mean, in practice, that the categorical rule the Court sought to define could be swallowed up by an essentially *ad hoc* exception. What is worse, courts would have to conduct this *ad hoc* inquiry in a strange, hypothetical fashion, asking what state courts would have decided about a common law nuisance case that was never brought. Consider, for example, a developer who buys land in 1970 and holds it in its natural state. Thirty years later, the State enacts development restrictions barring development of the land because it lies in a flood plain. As of 1970, there were no applicable state nuisance precedents regarding flood plain construction. Under the *Lucas* nuisance test, a court must ask whether a private or public nuisance case seeking to bar flood plain development would have succeeded in 1970, had such a suit been brought then, which, of course, it was not.[173]

source law for the common law of nuisance is probably most acute in cases involving alleged takings by the federal government on federal land. Would the existence of a compensation requirement for federal regulations depend on the common law of nuisance of the State where the claimant's property happens to be located? If so, the same federal regulation might require compensation in some States but not in others.

173. The one thing the majority did make plain was its hope and expectation that the South Carolina Supreme Court on remand would hold the common law nuisance exception inapplicable to the restrictions imposed by the Beachfront Management Act, and, in fact, the South Carolina Supreme Court did hold

C. Government Actions that are *Per Se* Not Takings

If we view government action as falling along a spectrum from formal exercises of eminent domain at one end to pure police power regulation at the other, then our first two examples of categorical treatment (permanent physical occupations and complete loss of economic value) can be seen as analogical extensions from formal exercises of eminent domain. Less well recognized is the fact that the Court has also started from the other end of the spectrum—pure police power regulation—and has identified several categorical rules where compensation is never required. Four categorical rules that share this feature are the nuisance exception, the forfeiture rule, the navigation servitude, and the conflagration rule.[174]

that the nuisance exception was inapplicable. *See* Lucas v. South Carolina Coastal Council, 424 S.E.2d 484 (S.C.1992).

174. It is almost certain that other categorical rules against takings liability are implicitly understood to exist and are likely, at some point, to be expressly identified as such. Taxes, for example, have always been assumed to be immune from challenge under the Takings Clause, although there is no holding of the Court to this effect. *See supra* Chapter IVB1 note 104. In addition, as we note in the next chapter, zoning regulations that preserve nonconforming uses and permit at least one form of development are virtually always upheld against takings challenges. Thus, cases falling in this category might also be appropriate candidates for *per se* treatment.

1. The Nuisance Exception

One categorical exemption has already been referred to in connection with the *Lucas* decision: regulations that track the common law of nuisance never give rise to takings liability. This is so even if the regulation has the effect of totally eliminating all economic value of the property. It would seem to follow *a fortiorari* from this (although the Court has not yet squarely so held) that regulations that track the common law of nuisance but do *not* eliminate all economic value also never give rise to takings liability.

What is unclear after *Lucas* is whether regulations that do not perfectly conform to the common law of nuisance, but regulate activity that is nuisance-like are also eligible for *per se* rule of immunity from takings liability. For example, leaving an abandoned open-pit mine in an unreclaimed state was not traditionally regarded as a nuisance in most States. But today, such activity is widely recognized as leaving an unsightly scar on the land and as posing potential hazards, such as ground water contamination. Is a statute that requires restoring open-pit mines to their natural contours after closure immune from challenge as a taking under the nuisance exception, or must it be assessed under the *ad hoc* standard?

A clue to what the answer is likely to be is provided by *Palazzolo*,[175] where the Court rejected a related categorical exception for legislative/regulatory restrictions on land that were in effect at the

175. Palazzolo v. Rhode Island, 533 U.S. 606 (2001).

time the claimant acquired title. Before *Palazzolo*, many courts and commentators had assumed that landowners were on notice of any restrictions in effect when they purchased, and thus could have no reasonable expectation of compensation; indeed, any compensation would be a windfall for the buyer to the extent that the purchase price already reflected a discount for regulatory restrictions.[176] In *Palazzolo*, however, the Court rejected a "blanket rule that purchasers with notice have no compensation right when a claim becomes ripe...."[177] Justice Scalia's concurrence went further, maintaining that "[t]he fact that a restriction existed at the time the purchaser took title ... should have no bearing upon the determination of whether the restriction is so substantial as to constitute a taking."[178]

At one level, *Palazzolo* makes the nuisance exception recognized in *Lucas* all the more puzzling. *Lucas* appears to justify the nuisance exception on grounds of imputed notice. The notion is that purchasers cannot reasonably expect to engage in activ-

176. *See, e.g.,* Wooten v. South Carolina Coastal Council, 333 S.C. 469, 471, 510 S.E.2d 716, 717 (1999) ("there is no compensable regulatory taking when the property was subject to the restriction on use when the property was acquired"); *see also* Gregory M. Stein, *Who Gets the Takings Claim? Change in Land Use Law, Pre-Enactment Owners, and Post-Enactment Buyers,* 61 OHIO ST. L.J. 89 (2000) ("State courts have shown little sympathy for ... [buyers of] property with full knowledge of the recent restrictions because they should have received a price discount that factored in the risks of buying regulated property.").

177. *Palazzolo,* 533 U.S. at 609.

178. *Id.* at 637 (Scalia, J., concurring).

ities that were already excluded from their title when it was acquired, or to obtain compensation when they are subsequently prevented from engaging in those activities. But read together, *Lucas* and *Palazzolo* hold that purchasers have no compensation claim if they have imputed notice of common law restrictions in the title, but may have a compensation claim if they have such notice of non-common law, legislative restrictions on title. For example, imagine two cases, both of which involve the purchase of property in a flood plain in 1970. In Case I, the state courts have held prior to 1970 that construction in a flood plain constitutes a public nuisance. In Case II, there are no common law precedents, but a pre–1970 statute specifically prohibits construction in a flood plain. Under *Lucas* and *Palazzolo*, if the State after 1970 seeks to bar construction on the flood plain, a takings claim would automatically be barred in Case I (pre-purchase common law restrictions) but not in Case II (pre-purchase statutory restrictions).

The Supreme Court has not adequately explained this differential treatment of common law and non-common law restrictions on title. Justice Kennedy's opinion in *Palazzolo* suggests that the difference stems from the fact that legislative enactments do not necessarily reflect "common, shared understandings of permissible limitations [on land use] derived from a State's legal tradition."[179] Although

179. *Id.* at 630. *See also* Phillips v. Washington Legal Found., 524 U.S. 156, 168 (1998) (ignoring state supreme court rules in

this is cryptic, perhaps what it means is that nearly everyone would agree that regulations prohibiting activity that would be regarded as a nuisance at common law fall within the police power, and hence do not require compensation. This, then, is an appropriate category to carve out for *per se* treatment. There is less consensus about whether regulations that go beyond the common law of nuisance (like requiring reclamation of open pit mines or barring development in a flood plain) should *never* give rise to a claim for compensation. These sorts of claims are thus best left to examination under the *ad hoc* balancing test. The objective of identifying categorical rules is to conserve on information costs and make cases easier to decide. For these purposes confining categorical rules to areas of broad consensus makes sense.

In any event, *Palazzolo* makes it likely (although by no means certain) that the Justices will eventually confine the categorical nuisance exception to regulations that track the common law, not just for cases that involve a complete loss of economic value (the *Lucas* situation), but for all purposes, *i.e.*, for cases in which the loss in value is only partial. Presumably, the fact that a regulation covers activity that is analogous to, but not identical with, a common law nuisance would continue to be a factor to consider under *ad hoc* review.

favor of common law precedents in defining property because the latter are part of the "background principles" of property law).

2. *Forfeitures*

Government forfeitures are a second category of actions that are subject to a *per se* non-taking rule. Forfeitures are often imposed when property is used in the commission of a crime or a public nuisance. For example, a house that the government proves has been used to distribute illegal narcotics may be forfeited to the government; the judgment of forfeiture transfers title to the government, which may then use the property or sell it and devote the proceeds to fund ongoing governmental operations. The Court has held that as long as the forfeiture proceeding satisfies statutory and due process requirements, it does not raise any question under the Takings Clause.[180] If the forfeiture is otherwise valid, the Court has explained, it results in a transfer of property from the owner to the government by operation of law, and "[t]he government may not be required to compensate an owner for property which it has already lawfully acquired under the exercise of governmental authority other than the power of eminent domain."[181]

This reasoning is unsatisfactory, because the same sentence could be uttered in support of the proposition that no exercise of the police power will ever result in requiring the government to compensate the owner of property, which is directly contrary to *Pennsylvania Coal*. But the result is justifiable on grounds similar to those that support the categorical nuisance exception: history and imputed

180. *See* Bennis v. Michigan, 516 U.S. 442, 452 (1996).

181. *Id.* at 452.

notice. The Court has observed that forfeitures have a long history, going back to the medieval law of deodands, which required the forfeiture of any chattel that was the immediate cause of a death.[182] Given this history, one can argue, as in the case of the implied limitation on title that forbids the commission of nuisances, that everyone acquires property with constructive notice that it will be subject to forfeiture if the owner allows it to be used in the commission of a crime or a public nuisance. Also, providing compensation for forfeitures, even in only a fraction of the cases in which they occur, would undermine the deterrent effect of an important law enforcement tool. Thus, it is reasonable to carve out a categorical rule that immunizes forfeitures from takings claims.[183]

3. *The Navigation Servitude*

A third categorical exception from takings liability consists of injuries to property caused by federal efforts to maintain and enhance navigable waterways. It has long been established that the federal

182. *See* J.W. Goldsmith, Jr., Grant Co. v. United States, 254 U.S. 505, 510 (1921).

183. Of course, a categorical rule against compensation for forfeitures might not apply to cases in which the court discerned the true legislative motivation as being a desire to expropriate property while avoiding the strictures of eminent domain, rather than punishment of criminal or otherwise clearly harmful conduct. In other words, the question remains whether government takings of property formally designated as forfeitures, but judicially understood as substantively something else, would fall outside a categorical rule against compensation.

government has a "navigation servitude" that permits it to regulate and keep clear the channels of navigable waterways, regardless of who owns the bed beneath the water. In *United States v. Cherokee Nation of Oklahoma*,[184] the U.S. Army Corps of Engineers undertook to improve navigation on the Arkansas River in Oklahoma, and in doing so damaged certain sand and gravel deposits that belonged to Indian tribes as owners of the river bed. The Court reversed the judgment of the lower court that a tribe's claim for just compensation should be resolved under a balancing test, holding that in these circumstances, "[n]o such 'balancing' is required."[185] The reasoning was similar to that invoked in the case of forfeitures: "The proper exercise of this power is not an invasion of any property rights in the stream or the lands underlying it, for the damage sustained does not result from taking property from riparian owners within the meaning of the Fifth Amendment but from the lawful exercise of a power to which the interests of riparian owners have always been subject."[186]

Although the Court's decision appears to rest on fiat, history and imputed notice again sustain the result. Government action to keep the channels of commerce free of obstructions has long been understood to lie near the core of the police power, and claims for compensation when property has been

184. 480 U.S. 700 (1987).

185. *Id.* at 703.

186. *Id.* at 704, *quoting* United States v. Rands, 389 U.S. 121, 123 (1967).

damaged by such efforts have been uniformly rejected. Persons who own land and minerals underneath navigable waters are presumably aware of this tradition, and thus cannot claim surprise if their property is injured by government efforts to maintain or enhance the waterway.

4. *The Conflagration Rule*

A final *per se* exception from takings liability is the "conflagration rule," which posits that the state is absolved from any duty to compensate for property destroyed to prevent the spread of fire to other property. Outside the military context, the Supreme Court has never directly confronted the question whether the government can be held liable for a taking when it sacrifices the property of A in order to save the property of B, C and D.[187] But it has recognized that the conflagration rule was an established feature of the common law.[188] And *Lucas* contains a dictum that acknowledges the destruction of buildings or other property to stop a fire—or

187. In cases arising in the theater of war, the Court has held that the government may destroy property owned by U.S. nationals in order to combat the spread of disease, *see* Juragua Iron Co. v. United States, 212 U.S. 297 (1909), or to prevent the property from falling into enemy hands, *see* United States v. Caltex, Inc., 344 U.S. 149 (1952).

188. *See* United States v. Pacific R. Co., 120 U.S. 227, 238–39 (1887); Bowditch v. Boston, 101 U.S. 16, 18–19 (1879). *See also* Respublica v. Sparhawk, 1 Dall. 357, 363 (Pa.1788) (pre-Fifth Amendment decision relying on conflagration rule to deny claim of compensation for personal property removed from city by Revolutionary War troops and then seized by British troops).

indeed "to forestall other grave threats to the lives and property of others"—would fall within yet another categorical exception from takings liability.[189]

At first blush, the conflagration rule seems to run counter to our general intuitions about takings. The government has singled out particular property for deliberate and complete destruction, in order to provide a benefit to the community at large. If the government must provide compensation for flooding caused by the closure of a government dam, or for property requisitioned for use by the military, why should the government not also be required to compensate owners when their property is destroyed to block the spread of fire or other contagion?

There are a variety of possible explanations for the exception. One is based on implicit *ex ante* compensation. The practice of allowing the government to destroy buildings in the path of fire significantly reduces the total amount of destruction caused by catastrophic fires. All owners thus receive implicit compensation in the form of reduced insurance rates for giving up the right to *ex post* compensation. Another is based on causation. If the claimant's property would have been engulfed by fire in any event, then the government's intervention should not be regarded as the cause if its demise. A third is based on an extension of the nuisance exception. Although an inert building is ordinarily not a nuisance, when approached by a raging fire it can be said to take on the characteristics of a tinder

189. *Lucas*, 505 U.S. at 1029 n.16.

box, and thus poses a nuisance-like threat to other buildings.[190] Finally, it has been argued that a categorical rule of no liability is necessary in order to make sure that fire officials do not hesitate before taking action that is clearly in the aggregate interest of the community. If fire officials are concerned that the government—or perhaps they personally— may be held liable for a large compensation award, they may not act with the requisite dispatch to avert a larger disaster.[191]

Whatever the ultimate justification for the conflagration rule, it has been around for a long time, has never been questioned, and has been characterized as falling squarely within the state's police power.[192] Thus, it too partakes of the general characteristics we have identified as giving rise to a categorical rule of no liability.

190. *See* WILLIAM A. FISCHEL, REGULATORY TAKINGS: LAW, ECONOMICS, AND POLITICS 357 (1995).

191. *See Respublica*, 1 Dall. at 363 (recounting the story that the Lord Mayor of London in 1666 hesitated to order the destruction of the Inns of Court without the consent of the judges, with the result that half of London burned down).

192. *Bowditch*, 101 U.S. at 19.

CHAPTER VI

TAKINGS: *AD HOC* REVIEW

The "takings" inquiry in most cases is resolved under a categorical rule. This is because most cases that arise under the Takings Clause involve condemnations pursuant to eminent domain authority, and condemnation implicitly, but categorically, is regarded as always a taking. If, however, we focus only on *regulatory* takings cases—those in which the government purports to act under the police power, but the property owner claims it should have proceeded by eminent domain—then we find that most cases are decided not by categorical rules but under a standard that the Supreme Court has acknowledged is *ad hoc*, fact-specific, and openly messy. This *ad hoc* review originated with the Court's decision in *Pennsylvania Coal Co. v. Mahon*,[193] but today is often called *Penn Central* review, after the decision that gave it its modern formulation, *Penn Central Transportation Co. v. City of New York*.[194]

Until recently, most proponents of an expanded regulatory takings doctrine have favored increased use of categorical rules, while those drawn to a narrow takings doctrine have argued that the *ad*

193. 260 U.S. 393 (1922).

194. 438 U.S. 104 (1978).

hoc approach should predominate. This alignment reflects the fact that most judges have used the flexibility afforded by *ad hoc* review to find that challenged government action is not a taking. But this could change; the very flexibility afforded by the *ad hoc* approach could just as easily be used to reach the opposite result. One court in particular—the United States Court of Federal Claims that hears takings claims against the federal government—has shown signs of increased willingness to use the *ad hoc* approach to find regulatory takings.[195] What this tells us is simply that *ad hoc* review gives great discretion to judges. Whether particular advocates favor categorical or *ad hoc* review will largely depend on whether they agree with the way judges currently exercise their discretionary power to say whether government action is a taking.

In this chapter we begin by summarizing what *Pennsylvania Coal* and *Penn Central* teach us about *ad hoc* review of the "takings" question. We then consider in more detail the menu of the factors that

---

195. *See, e.g.,* Florida Rock Indus. v. United States, 21 Cl.Ct. 161, 170 (1990), *remanded,* 18 F.3d 1560 (Fed.Cir.1994) (holding that wetlands regulation constituted a regulatory taking under *ad hoc* approach); Loveladies Harbor, Inc. v. United States, 21 Cl.Ct. 153 (1990) (finding a taking under *ad hoc* approach), *aff'd on other grounds,* 28 F.3d 1171 (Fed.Cir.1994). *See generally* Basil H. Mattingly, *Forum over Substance: The Empty Ritual of Balancing in Regulatory Takings Jurisprudence,* 36 Willamette L. Rev. 695, 746 (2000) (concluding, based on an examination of approximately 100 takings cases, that "[I]f the private party does not believe that she can convince a court to dispose of the case through one of the *per se* rules, [she] is much better off in the claims court.").

have been recognized as bearing on this inquiry, and suggest how these factors may function in much the same way as the categorical rules by helping us sort government actions into those that are more like condemnations and those that are more like traditional police power regulations. We conclude with a note about takings challenges to public utility rate orders, an area in which the Court has also applied an *ad hoc* approach, but one that invokes different factors than the *ad hoc* review associated with *Pennsylvania Coal* and *Penn Central*.

A. *Pennsylvania Coal* and *Penn Central*

The Supreme Court's decision in *Pennsylvania Coal*, as we have seen, is primarily significant because of its explicit recognition of the regulatory takings doctrine. But *Pennsylvania Coal* was also the first decision to articulate and apply an *ad hoc* approach to determining when a police power regulation should be regarded as a taking. The case involved a Pennsylvania statute protecting surface owners of land from subsidence caused by the mining of coal beneath their property. The Pennsylvania Coal Company, which owned the rights to mine the coal, challenged the statute as an uncompensated taking of the pillars of coal that would have to remain in place in order to prevent damage to the surface.

The Supreme Court agreed with the Coal Company that the subsidence law was a taking, and in so
ruling produced famous dueling opinions from Justice Holmes, writing for the majority, and Justice
Brandeis, in dissent. Writing in his characteristical-
ly pithy style, Justice Holmes said that whether a
government regulation is a taking is a "question of
degree—and therefore cannot be disposed of by
general propositions."[196] The "general rule," he
said, is "that while property may be regulated to a
certain extent, if regulation goes too far it will be
recognized as a taking."[197] Whether the government
has gone "too far," he added, will depend "on the
particular facts" of each case. In other words, Justice Holmes endorsed a case-by-case or *ad hoc* approach to deciding regulatory takings challenges.

The Holmes' opinion, of course, pointed to certain
factors that caused the majority to conclude that
this particular Pennsylvania statute went "too far."
One factor mentioned was diminution in value
caused by the regulation. Justice Holmes characterized the extent of the loss as "great" because the
statute rendered the pillars of coal needed to support the surface of no commercial value. A second
factor was whether the regulation served to prevent
a harm to the general public. Justice Holmes concluded that the statute did not have this effect,
because subsidence damage to a single private
house is not a public nuisance, and any injury to
third parties could be avoided by providing notice of

196. *Pennsylvania Coal*, 260 U.S. at 416.

197. *Id.* at 415.

impending mining activity. A third factor was that the statute appeared to confer a benefit on surface owners and a burden on owners of coal in place, and thus could not be said to secure "an average reciprocity of advantage" among all affected property owners.[198] Finally, Justice Holmes emphasized that the regulation effectively destroyed recognized property and contract rights: the statute "purports to abolish what is recognized in Pennsylvania as an estate in land—a very valuable estate—and what is declared by the Court below to be a contract hitherto binding the plaintiffs."[199]

Justice Brandeis disagreed with the majority's application of each of these factors. The diminution in value was probably not that great, Justice Brandeis argued, if one considered the value of "the whole property" rather than some segment or subset of the property like the value of the coal kept in place by the restriction.[200] Justice Brandeis also thought that the public purpose behind the regulation was substantial; as he saw it, the statute was designed to prevent a "noxious use" of property that was properly characterized as a public nuisance.[201] As to reciprocity of advantage, Justice Brandeis acknowledged that this might be an important consideration under a statute that sought

198. *Id.* at 415.

199. *Id.* at 414; *see also id.* at 413 ("As applied to this case the statute is admitted to destroy previously existing rights of property and contract.").

200. *Id.* at 419 (dissenting opinion).

201. *Id.* at 417 (dissenting opinion).

to confer a benefit on landowners, but not where the law was designed "to protect the public from detriment and danger."[202] Finally, Justice Brandeis argued that the fact the regulation abrogated recognized rights of property and contract was not necessarily dispositive, citing in support decisions holding that individuals cannot remove their rights from the police power "by making a contract about them."[203]

The enduring significance of the debate between Justices Holmes and Brandeis almost certainly does not lie in their disagreement about how the various factors cited by the majority should be applied to mining subsidence regulations. Years later, in *Keystone Bituminous Coal Ass'n v. DeBenedictis*,[204] the Supreme Court upheld against a takings challenge another Pennsylvania anti-subsidence statute that closely resembled the statute in *Pennsylvania Coal*, and, in so doing, relied upon much the same reasoning as the Brandeis dissent.[205] Thus, Justice Brandeis's views about the application of these factors may be closer to those of the modern Court than were Justice Holmes's views.

What is of greater significance is that Justice Holmes and Justice Brandeis agreed, at least in

202. *Id.* at 422 (dissenting opinion).

203. *Id.* at 421 (quoting Hudson County Water Co. v. McCarter, 209 U.S. 349, 357 (1908)).

204. 480 U.S. 470 (1987).

205. The Court, however, did not purport to overrule *Pennsylvania Coal*, and instead distinguished (rather unconvincingly) the statute before it from the statute at issue in *Pennsylvania Coal. See id.* at 481–502.

broad terms, about the legal relevance of a number of factors. Both agreed that the extent of diminution in value and whether the government is seeking to abate a public nuisance are relevant factors, and both agreed that whether a regulation secures an average reciprocity of advantage among property owners is sometimes relevant. Even with respect to the fourth factor—whether the statute destroys previously existing property or contract rights recognized by state law—Justice Brandeis confined his disagreement mostly to whether destruction of contract rights should be deemed a taking.

In 1978, the Supreme Court decided *Penn Central Transportation Co. v. City of New York*,[206] the decision most often cited today as providing the governing doctrinal structure for takings cases where a categorical rule does not apply.[207] The case involved a takings challenge to a New York City landmark designation that prevented the owners of the Penn Central Station, with its famous Beaux Arts design, from constructing a new office building in the air space above the station. In rejecting the challenge, the Court reaffirmed that the takings inquiry entails "essentially *ad hoc*, factual inquiries."[208] Writing for the majority, Justice Brennan cited three factors as being of particular importance in giving structure to these inquires: (1) the diminution in

206. 438 U.S. 104 (1978).

207. *See, e.g.,* Palazzolo v. Rhode Island, 533 U.S. 606, 630 (2001) (reaffirming applicability of *Penn Central* in absence of total diminution in value).

208. *Penn Central*, 438 U.S. at 124–25.

value of the property attributable to the challenged regulation; (2) the extent to which the regulation interferes with the owner's distinct investment-backed expectations; and (3) the character of the government action.[209]

Although Justice Brennan presented these factors as a restatement of precedent, they are, in fact, quite different from the factors relied upon in *Pennsylvania Coal*. Only the first factor—diminution in value—was carried over from *Pennsylvania Coal*. The other three factors mentioned by the majority in *Pennsylvania Coal* were either ignored or relegated to secondary consideration. In their place, the *Penn Central* majority advanced two new factors— investment-backed expectations and the character of the government action—that made their debut in the *Penn Central* case itself.

The *Penn Central* majority applied its three factors to conclude that the landmark regulation was a permissible exercise of the police power and hence did not trigger any obligation to pay compensation. First, according to the majority, the landmark designation did not significantly diminish the value of the company's property. In particular, the law did not prevent the company from earning a reasonable rate of return on its existing investment in the

209. *Id*. It should be noted that *Penn Central* did not clearly differentiate among these three factors, nor did it suggest that they form some definitive "test." The treatment of the three factors as distinct elements of an *ad hoc* test, with attribution to *Penn Central*, began with Kaiser Aetna v. United States, 444 U.S. 164, 175 (1979), and was then perpetuated in later decisions of the Court.

station.[210] Second, because the only historical use of the site had been as a station and because the company had not actually invested any money in construction above the station, the regulation did not interfere with what the majority characterized as the owner's "primary expectation" regarding the parcel.[211] Third, the majority rejected the argument that the building prohibition was analogous to a physical invasion of airspace, and instead analogized the regulation to run-of-the-mill, widely accepted zoning regulations.

Justice Rehnquist's dissenting opinion did not so much take issue with the majority's analysis of these three factors as it urged that the case be resolved under the traditional *Pennsylvania Coal* factors. Justice Rehnquist argued, first, that the City was not seeking to prohibit conduct "dangerous to the safety, health, or welfare of others"; rather, it sought to provide a benefit in the form of preserving a pleasing façade.[212] Second, the law singled out a very small percentage of property owners in New York City for unique burdens, and hence could not be said to secure the "average reciprocity of advantage" mentioned in *Pennsylva-*

210. The Court's reference to a reasonable return on investment implicitly invokes the public utility cases, discussed *infra* Ch VIC. This is one of the few cross-references in the Supreme Court's decisions between the *ad hoc* review employed in land use cases and the *ad hoc* standard developed in public utility cases.

211. 438 U.S. at 136.

212. *Id.* at 145 (dissenting opinion).

nia Coal.[213] Third, Justice Rehnquist observed that the regulation had the effect of transferring a servitude to the city, which is a type of property right that is often acquired by purchase or condemnation.[214]

It is difficult to know what caused the shift in the factors deemed relevant to an *ad hoc* analysis between *Pennsylvania Coal* and *Penn Central*. But the most obvious explanation is that each of the three factors that were downplayed in *Penn Central*—whether the regulation targets a noxious use of property, secures an average reciprocity of advantage, and abrogates a recognized property right—inconveniently suggested that the preservation order should have been deemed a taking. So Justice Brennan demoted these factors and instead elevated two new factors—investment-backed expectations and the character of the government action—that pointed toward the conclusion that there was no taking. If this analysis is correct, then courts probably have placed too much emphasis on the three "*Penn Central* factors" as being a definitive statement of the variables that are relevant in considering whether a regulation effects a taking. The relevant factors should be gleaned from a broader survey of the Court's regulatory takings decisions.

Decisions subsequent to *Penn Central* add little to our understanding of *ad hoc* review. The most important development in takings law after *Penn Cen-*

213. *Id.* at 147 (dissenting opinion).

214. *Id.* at 143, 146, 152 n.14 (dissenting opinion).

tral has been the emergence of the categorical rules, which is itself something of an implicit condemnation of the *ad hoc* approach. In those cases that have continued to apply *ad hoc* review, sometimes the Court has repeated the three *Penn Central* factors as if they are a fixed formula, other times, the Court has paid little heed to the *Penn Central* factors.[215] Sometimes the Court has given one particular factor greater weight than other factors, other times it has not.[216] It would dignify the approach too much to describe it as a multi-factoral test or even a balancing test. All one can say for certain is that the method is *ad hoc*, meaning that a variety of factors of uncertain priority or weight are potentially relevant, and there is no fixed method or procedure for relating these factors to each other or to the final determination whether a regulation is a taking.

B. Restating the Relevant Factors

Perhaps the place to begin in seeking a more comprehensive understanding of the elements that are relevant to an *ad hoc* takings analysis is to

215. *Compare* PruneYard Shopping Ctr. v. Robins, 447 U.S. 74, 83 (1980) (reciting and applying the three *Penn Central* factors) *with* Webb's Fabulous Pharmacies, Inc. v. Beckwith, 449 U.S. 155 (1980) (holding that a State's appropriation of interest on interpleader fund was a taking without discussing the *Penn Central* factors).

216. See, for example, the discussion below about the inconsistent application of the investment-backed expectations factor.

synthesize the factors relied upon in *Pennsylvania Coal* and *Penn Central*, which remain the Court's two leading decisions on the nature of *ad hoc* review. We can then ask whether each of these factors makes sense as a variable for differentiating between those actions that should be taken under the power of eminent domain and those that may proceed under the police power. Altogether, the Court mentioned six factors in the two decisions as being relevant to whether any particular exercise of the police power "goes too far" and should be regarded as a taking. These are, from both *Pennsylvania Coal* and *Penn Central*: (1) the extent of diminution in value of the property caused by the regulation; from *Penn Central*: (2) whether the regulation upsets reasonable investment-backed expectations; and (3) the character of the government action; and from *Pennsylvania Coal*: (4) whether the regulation is of a noxious use of property; (5) whether the regulation provides an average reciprocity of advantage among property owners; and (6) whether the regulation destroys a recognized property right.

Significantly, several of these factors reflect less extreme versions of the Court's categorical rules considered in the previous chapter. Diminutions in value are a less extreme instance of complete loss of value, which *Lucas v. South Carolina Coastal Council*[217] holds are always a taking (unless an exception applies). The character of the government action, with its focus on government invasions of property, is a less extreme form of permanent physical occu-

217.   505 U.S. 1003 (1992).

pations, which *Loretto v. Teleprompter Manhattan CATV Corp.*[218] holds are always a taking. And regulation of noxious uses of property includes as a subset regulations that track the common law of nuisance, which *Lucas* says are never a taking. This overlap between the Court's categorical rules and its *ad hoc* factors suggests that, as in the case of the categorical rules, the *ad hoc* factors may function as proxies that help situate the challenged government action along a spectrum from traditional exercises of eminent domain at one end to traditional police power regulations at the other.

Indeed, a plausible case can be made that each of the six *ad hoc* factors identifies a characteristic that is commonly associated with either condemnation of property or police power regulation. Three factors— diminution in value, the character of the government action (invasion versus use regulation), and whether the action destroys a recognized property right—plausibly can be seen as proxies for action that is functionally equivalent to condemnation. Three other factors—whether the regulation targets a noxious use of property, whether the regulation preserves an average reciprocity of advantage among property owners, and whether the regulation interferes with reasonable investment-backed expectations—plausibly can be seen as proxies for actions that bear the indicia of police power regulations.

None of this is to suggest that *ad hoc* review can be transformed into a neat algorithm in which

218. 458 U.S. 419 (1982).

factors on one side or the other are toted up, or that
it can approach even the degree of certainty of the
Court's categorical rules. Even if we correctly cata-
logue all the factors (and we would caution that
there may be other factors courts will identify as
being relevant to the regulatory takings analysis), it
would still be necessary to determine the relative
weight of the different factors, something that the
current state of the case law does not permit. In
addition, as the law now stands, each of these
factors is subject to diverse interpretations in almost any case. Thus, although we believe courts
should and often in fact do consider a broader list of
factors than the three recited in *Penn Central*, there
is every prospect that *ad hoc* review will remain
highly indeterminate, and hence discretionary and
unpredictable. Let us briefly consider each of the six
factors in somewhat greater detail.

1. Diminution in Value

The factor that seems most securely grounded in
the decisions—it is mentioned in both *Pennsylvania
Coal* and in *Penn Central*—is the extent to which
the regulation has diminished the value of the
claimant's property. Diminution in value is a plausible but imperfect proxy for government actions that
should proceed by eminent domain rather than the
police power. Most condemnations result in a large
financial loss to the condemned property owner,
and most police regulations result in much more
modest costs to property owners. Consequently, ac-

tions that result in a large diminution in value are more likely to resemble condemnations and actions that result in small declines in value are more likely to resemble police regulations. There are, however, exceptions to these generalizations. Partial takings by condemnation sometimes entail little or no financial loss, and, as we shall see in the next chapter, may result in no compensation under the offsetting benefits rule. And some police power measures or tax provisions can generate very large financial losses. Diminution in value is thus a crude proxy for distinguishing between eminent domain and police power measures.

Perhaps the most commonly asked question in regulatory takings law is: How much diminution in value is enough to qualify as a taking? We know from *Lucas* that if the regulation causes a 100 percent diminution in value, it is a taking *per se* (at least if the common law nuisance exception does not apply). Short of a 100 percent loss in value, however, the degree of diminution is just one factor to be considered under the *ad hoc* approach. Presumably, the closer the diminution gets to 100 percent, the stronger this factor points toward the conclusion that the regulation is a taking. However, neither the Supreme Court nor the lower courts have developed any clear benchmarks as to what percentage diminution gives rise to a presumption in favor of a finding that there has been a taking.[219] Presumably,

219. The Court of Federal Claims has come closest to developing a clear jurisprudence in this respect, although, as a federal trial court, its decisions are not very authoritative. First, the

this is because no two cases will present exactly the same mix of other factors, and so focusing on any particular percentage as being of special significance would be misleading.

The most vexing problem associated with diminution in value, as discussed in the last chapter in connection with the total economic wipeout test, is how one defines the relevant parcel of property—the denominator—for purposes of computing the percentage diminution. *Penn Central* follows Justice Brandeis's dissent in *Pennsylvania Coal* in rejecting the division of a "single parcel" of property into discrete physical segments in order to determine "whether rights in a particular segment have been entirely abrogated."[220] But neither *Penn Central* nor subsequent decisions answer the question how one defines a "single parcel," and this can be key to

court of claims has articulated the principle that the plaintiff's initial burden is to produce evidence of diminution in value, and then the burden of production (but not the burden of persuasion) shifts to the government to identify some market value remaining in the property at issue. *See* Florida Rock Indus. v. United States, 21 Cl.Ct. 161, 170 (1990), *rev'd on other grounds*, 18 F.3d 1560 (Fed.Cir.1994); Loveladies Harbor v. United States, 21 Cl.Ct. 153, 158 (Cl.Ct.1990), *aff'd*, 28 F.3d 1171 (Fed.Cir.1994). Second, extreme, but not truly total diminutions in value receive essentially the same treatment as 100 percent diminutions in value. *See Loveladies Harbor*, 28 F.3d at 1174 (99 percent diminution in value is equivalent to deprivation of all economically viable use). Of course, because of the malleability in defining the denominator—that is, the scope of the property interests at issue—courts facing the same facts often could characterize the same regulation as effecting a range of percentages of diminution in value.

220.   438 U.S. at 130.

determining not only whether a total taking has occurred but also the percentage diminution in value where less than 100 percent of the value has been lost.

Imagine, for example, that before its passenger station was designated a landmark, the Penn Central Company had transferred the air rights over one half of the station to a wholly-owned subsidiary and sold off the remaining air rights to an unrelated entity. What then would be the relevant parcel(s), for purposes of a takings claim: each of the individual transferred air rights alone, the station plus all the air rights, the station plus the air rights held by the subsidiary, or just the station? Suppose the station is worth $50 million and each of the air-right grants are worth $20 million. Faced with a regulation that prohibits all development of the air rights, the diminution in value could be either (1) 20/20 or 100 percent; (2) 40/ 90 or 44 percent; (3) 20/70 or 29 percent; or (4) 0/50 or zero percent.

Penn Central addressed another thorny issue in assessing diminution in value—whether transferable development rights (TDRs) or other benefits allocated to an owner as part of a regulatory system should count in calculating diminution in value. The New York City regulations in *Penn Central* allowed the company to transfer its development rights in the airspace over the station to other nearby parcels, in effect permitting more development of the other parcels than otherwise would be allowed under applicable zoning rules. Justice Brennan said that the TDRs "undoubtedly mitigate whatever financial burdens the law has imposed on appellants and, for that reason, are to be taken into account in considering the impact of the regulation."[221] Similarly, in *Suitum v. Tahoe Regional Planning Agency*,[222] the Court suggested that TDRs are relevant in determining the diminution in value attributable to a regulation. The dissent in *Penn Central* and Justice Scalia concurring in *Suitum* disagreed, arguing that "[p]utting TDRs on the taking rather than the just compensation side of the equation . . . is a clever, albeit transparent, device that seeks to take advantage of a peculiarity of our Takings jurisprudence: Whereas once there is a taking, the Constitution requires just (i.e., full) compensation . . . [a] regulatory taking generally does not occur so long as the land retains substantial (albeit not its full) value. . . . "[223]

The debate over whether TDRs and other regulatory benefits should count in assessing diminution in value boils down to the conceptual question of what "the regulation" is for the purposes of determining whether a regulation of property effects a taking. In general, those who would afford limited protection for takings construe "the regulation" broadly to include benefits such as TDRs, just as they construe "single parcel" broadly to include interests and areas unaffected by regulatory restric-

221. *Id.* at 137.

222. 520 U.S. 725, 737–42 (1997).

223. *Id.* at 746 (Scalia, J., concurring) (emphasis omitted). *See also Penn Central*, 438 U.S. at 138, 150–51 (Rehnquist, J., dissenting).

tions. Conversely, those who favor an expansive Takings Clause construe "the regulation" to exclude benefits such as TDRs, just as they narrowly construe the "single parcel" to include only areas affected by regulatory restrictions. The case law offers no more clear guidance for determining whether "the regulation" should be construed broadly or narrowly than it does for whether a "single parcel" should be construed broadly or narrowly.

2. The Character of the Government Action

The Court in *Penn Central* also held that the "character of the governmental action" is relevant in *ad hoc* review. The Court offered only one example of how the character of the action matters: If the action constitutes a physical invasion by the government, then a taking "may more readily be found ... than when interference arises from some public program adjusting the benefits and burdens of economic life to promote the common good."[224] The invasion versus use-regulation distinction is a good proxy for identifying actions that should proceed by eminent domain, for the reasons discussed in the last chapter in connection with *Loretto*'s categorical rule for permanent government occupations. Condemnations result in a transfer of possession of property from the owner to the condemning authority. A government-authorized invasion also displaces the owner from possession, and thus shares a critical attribute of a condemnation. Regulations of the use of property, in contrast, do not

224. *Penn Central*, 438 U.S. at 124.

interfere with possession, and hence lack this critical feature of condemnation.

One puzzle presented by this factor is why the Court in *Penn Central* spoke in general terms about the "character of the government action" rather than simply asking whether the government has authorized an invasion of the property. Are there other types of government action besides invasions that also strongly suggest the government should proceed by eminent domain rather than police power regulation?

One possible candidate would be regulations that abrogate a property owner's right to exclude others. Several decisions subsequent to *Penn Central* have said that regulations that abrogate an owner's "right to exclude" are an especially severe type of action, in effect raising a red flag under the Takings Clause.[225] But the right to exclude can be seen as simply the flip side of government-authorized invasions of property. Abrogate the right to exclude and invasions, either by the government or sanctioned by the government, may follow. Thus, abrogation of the right to exclude does not necessarily present a different "character of action" than the type of action singled out in *Penn Central*.

225. *See, e.g.*, Dolan v. City of Tigard, 512 U.S. 374, 384 (1994); Ruckelshaus v. Monsanto Co., 467 U.S. 986, 1011 (1984); Kaiser Aetna v. United States, 444 U.S. 164, 176 (1979); *cf.* College Sav. Bank v. Florida Prepaid Postsecondary Educ. Expense Bd., 527 U.S. 666, 673 (1999) (observing that the right to exclude is the "hallmark" of private property). *But see* Prune-Yard Shopping Ctr. v. Robins, 447 U.S. 74 (1980) (holding that state court decision abrogating the right to exclude political demonstrators from privately-owned shopping center was not a taking).

Other decisions have suggested that government abrogation of the right to pass on property to one's heirs is an especially significant type of action strongly suggestive of a taking.[226] At least where the right to devise and descent of land have been totally abrogated, the Court has suggested that *ad hoc* review should tilt in favor of requiring compensation.[227] The Court has said that the right to devise, like the right to exclude, is especially important or fundamental to property ownership. At the same time, however, the Court has acknowledged that government regulation of devise and descent generally is permissible without compensation.[228]

Whether abrogation of the right to transmit property on death should be on a par with physical invasion in terms of identifying actions that should proceed by eminent domain is doubtful. Rights of devise and descent are created by law and have always been subject to extensive legislative regulation. Traditionally, as long as such legislation does not abrogate "vested" rights of inheritance, there had been no suggestion that the government must proceed by eminent domain.[229] To date, however,

226. *See* Babbitt v. Youpee, 519 U.S. 234 (1997); Hodel v. Irving, 481 U.S. 704 (1987).

227. *See Hodel*, 481 U.S. at 716.

228. *Id.* at 717–18.

229. *See, e.g.*, Randall v. Kreiger, 90 U.S. (23 Wall.) 137, 148 (1874) (concluding that legislature is free to modify dower estate until such time as wife becomes a widow and estate is vested).

the Court's decisions in this area have not been sufficiently clear to say that they stand for the proposition that rights of devise and descent are entitled to special consideration.

Another puzzle presented by the character of the government action variable is how government invasion can serve both as a categorical takings rule under *Loretto* and just one factor under the *ad hoc* approach. Of course, *Penn Central* (1978) was decided before *Loretto* (1982). But the Court on many occasions since *Loretto* has reaffirmed that the "character of the government action," *i.e.*, invasion, is a relevant factor under the *ad hoc* approach, without making any effort to clarify the overlapping role of the invasion variable under the two approaches.

The most obvious explanation for the overlap is that the two tests require different degrees of invasion. The categorical rule of *Loretto* requires a *permanent* physical occupation, whereas the character of the government action factor requires only a physical invasion. This suggests that we can harmonize *Penn Central* and *Loretto* by reading them as establishing a three-part analytic structure: permanent physical invasions by the government are *per se* or categorical takings; nonpermanent physical invasions are subject to heightened, albeit still non-categorical, review of the *ad hoc* sort;[230] and

230. Kaiser Aetna v. United States, 444 U.S. 164, 180 (1979), indicates that the balance in physical invasion cases tilts toward a finding of a taking even "if the Government physically invades only an easement in property."

noninvasive regulations, all else being equal, are subject to the most deferential form of *ad hoc* review.

Another possible explanation for the overlap is that it allows courts to consider the invasiveness of the government action as a factor when, for some reason, the categorical rule for permanent occupations does not apply. In post-*Loretto* cases, the Court has held that where the original occupation was voluntarily agreed to by the owner, subsequent government regulation that perpetuates the relationship is not a government-compelled permanent occupation.[231] For example, if a property owner rents land to a tenant, and the government later limits the rent that tenant must pay and the grounds on which the tenant can be evicted, the Court has said *Loretto*'s categorical rule does not apply. It may be, however, that this sort of regulatory scheme, by forcing the owner to allow an unwanted tenant to remain on the land, is sufficiently invasive in nature that the character of the government action should be considered a relevant factor under an *ad hoc* analysis.

3. *Destruction of Recognized Rights of Property*

Pennsylvania Coal laid great stress on the fact that the law protecting surface owners against mining subsidence had the effect of extinguishing a

231. *See* Yee v. Escondido, 503 U.S. 519 (1992); FCC v. Florida Power Corp., 480 U.S. 245 (1987).

distinctive "support estate" recognized by the law of Pennsylvania. Later decisions also placed great weight on whether a regulation has the effect of destroying or compelling the transfer of a recognized property right.[232] It is unclear today whether this factor still commands the Court's allegiance as a relevant consideration under an *ad hoc* analysis. In *Penn Central*, the majority placed little significance on the fact that "air rights" were an interest in land recognized by New York law. And in *Keystone Bituminous Coal*, which involved the same "third estate" in support rights that the Court found had been extinguished by the law in *Pennsylvania Coal*, the majority again placed relatively little weight on this factor.

Still, there are a number of post-*Penn Central* decisions where the extinction or forced transfer of property rights appears to have played a role in the Court's analysis. In *Kaiser Aetna v. United States*,[233] for example, the Court appeared to be moved by the perception that the regulation opening a marina to public navigation was the functional equivalent of forcing the transfer of a public easement. And *Ruckelshaus v. Monsanto Co.*[234] found that a regulation created a taking when it forced disclosure of information that had the effect of extinguishing a common law trade secret. So it is quite possible that

232. *See, e.g.*, Armstrong v. United States, 364 U.S. 40, 48 (1960) (holding destruction of materialman liens, found to be a distinct right of property, was a taking).

233. 444 U.S. at 164, 179–80 (1979).

234. 467 U.S. 986 (1984).

this factor lives on in practice, even if it has not been explicitly recognized in recent Supreme Court opinions summarizing the elements of *ad hoc* review.

Whether government action results in the destruction of a recognized property right should in theory serve as a good proxy for actions that ought to proceed by eminent domain rather than the police power. Condemnation always results in the transfer of a distinct property right from the owner to the government or its agent. Thus, regulations that have the effect of destroying or compelling the transfer of a recognized property right share a critical attribute of actions taken pursuant to the power of eminent domain.

The central difficulty presented by any inquiry into whether a government action has destroyed a recognized property right is what we mean by "property right." On the one hand, if we limit this to mean just the standard units of ownership—fee simples, leases, affirmative easements, patents, mineral rights, and so forth—then this factor would appear to duplicate *Lucas's* categorical rule for regulations that eliminate all economic value of property. A regulation that destroys or forces a transfer of a fee simple, a lease, etc. would presumably violate the *Lucas* total wipeout rule and hence would be a taking *per se*. On the other hand, if we interpret "property right" to include incidents of property, such as the rights to transfer, to devise and descend, and to use property in various ways, then virtually every regulation of property could be said to destroy or compel the transfer of some property right. Interpreting property right to include every incident of property in effect creates a version of the problem of conceptual severance, discussed in Chapter IV in connection with the definition of private property.

The Court's decision in *Pennsylvania Coal* illustrates the dilemma. The majority was impressed by the fact that the Pennsylvania law had the effect of nullifying previously negotiated waivers of support rights. Such waivers were commonly bought and sold in conjunction with transfers of mineral rights.[235] In functional terms, these waivers were servitudes that ran with the ownership of the mineral estate and the surface estate, adding an additional incident to the rights of the mineral estate owner—the right to mine to the point of causing subsidence of the surface, ordinarily barred by the common law of subjacent support rights.

In some respects, waivers of support rights have the characteristics of a property right: They can be bought and sold, they run with the land, and they are formally reflected in deeds to the surface and the mineral estate. But in other respects, they lack the characteristics of full-fledged property: They create only personal rights and duties between the owner of the minerals and the surface, and they are not exchanged on a stand-alone basis independently of some other property right. There would seem to

235. *See* Carol M. Rose, Mahon *Reconstructed: Why The Takings Issue is Still a Muddle*, 57 S. Cal. L. Rev. 561, 563–64 (1984).

be no clearly correct answer as to whether we label such waivers of support rights a "property right" or something else.

It might be possible to fashion a solution to this dilemma. For purposes of *ad hoc* review, we could decide to count as a "property right" any interest in property that is exchangeable and that runs to successors in interest, but not insist that it be exchangeable on a stand-alone basis. This would be broader than the definition of "private property" proposed in Chapter IV, because it would include covenants running with the land as well as more conventional types of property. Thus, the destruction factor would not simply duplicate the *Lucas* categorical rule. But such a definition would also be sufficiently narrow that it would not include every possible incident of property or contract about the use of property. Consequently, it would also avoid the more extreme problems of conceptual severance. Whether such a solution would ever be adopted is highly conjectural. The case law that invokes the destruction of rights factor is underdeveloped, and as things stand today, shows few signs of developing any further.

4. *Regulation of Noxious Uses*

The most enduring factor under an *ad hoc* analysis is whether the regulation seeks to abate a noxious use of property. This factor was introduced in the Nineteenth Century in *Mugler v. Kansas*,[236]

236. 123 U.S. 623, 668–69 (1887).

where the Court observed that "all property in this country is held under the implied obligation that the owner's use of it shall not be injurious to the community."[237] Similar reasoning was applied in a variety of cases before and after *Pennsylvania Coal*,[238] and of course both the majority and dissenting opinions in that case recognized that the state may regulate public nuisances under its police power. The noxious use factor temporarily receded from view in *Penn Central*, but was soon restored to a place of prominence in *Keystone Bituminous Coal*, which discussed the noxious use exception at length and reaffirmed the Court's "hesitance to a find a taking when the State merely restrains uses of property that are tantamount to public nuisances."[239] And as previously discussed, *Lucas* recognizes an apparently categorical exception from takings liability when the regulation is designed to abate a common law nuisance. This clearly implies that the nuisance-abating nature of a regulation would, at the very least, be a highly relevant factor under an *ad hoc* analysis.

Asking whether the government action seeks to abate a noxious use of property is a good proxy for

237. *Id.* at 665. The "injurious" use at issue in *Mugler* was operating a brewery, which the State had outlawed in an early prohibition statute.

238. *See, e.g.*, Hadacheck v. Sebastian, 239 U.S. 394 (1915) (upholding law barring operation of brick mill in residential area as valid exercise of police power); Miller v. Schoene, 276 U.S. 272 (1928) (upholding order to destroy diseased cedar trees to prevent infection of nearby orchard as a valid exercise of the police power).

239. *Keystone Bituminous*, 480 U.S. at 491.

traditional police power measures. Whatever its outer limits, the police power, at its core, has always been understood to include the power to control public nuisances and other activities that can be said to be harmful to the public. Thus, other things being equal, if the government action is designed to abate a noxious use of property, we can be fairly confident that it falls within the conventional domain of the police power, and thus does not qualify as a taking.[240]

Although something like the noxious use factor is securely established in takings jurisprudence, there is great uncertainty as to how it should be defined. At one extreme, courts could adopt the position that *Lucas* staked out for its categorical exception to takings liability, and define "noxious use" narrowly to mean activities that would be recognized to be nuisances at common law. At the other extreme, one could interpret "noxious use" broadly to mean simply that the regulation is designed to advance some legitimate public purpose. Both extremes should probably be rejected.

Confining the noxious use exception to common law nuisances is difficult to square with the historical run of the cases, which appear to admit of much more flexibility in their characterization of harm-

240. For an extended argument that the Court's takings cases can best be reconciled as requiring compensation for intentional takings unless the claimant is engaged in conduct the public would regard as wrongful, *see* Andrea L. Peterson, *The Takings Clause: In Search of Underlying Principles Part II— Takings as Intentional Deprivations of Property Without Moral Justification*, 78 CAL. L. REV. 55 (1990).

creating activity. The Court has recognized that breweries, infected cedar trees, open quarries, and mining coal under property without support rights can all be regarded as noxious uses, even though there is some doubt as to whether any of these activities would be regarded as nuisances at common law.[241] And modern environmental laws often regulate property in ways that would not have been possible under the common law, yet the Court has never suggested that these laws are not proper police power measures.[242]

On the other hand, defining noxious use to be coterminous with any legitimate public interest would sap the concept of any meaningful content, and make regulatory takings analysis equivalent to due process rationality review.[243] The noxious use factor should therefore, at a minimum, be limited to regulations that seek to abate harmful spillovers, rather than extended to any regulation that has

241. *See Mugler* , 123 U.S. 623 (breweries); *Miller v. Schoene*, 276 U.S. 272 (infected cedar trees); Goldblatt v. Town of Hempstead, 369 U.S. 590 (1962) (open quarry); *Keystone Bituminous Coal*, 480 U.S. 470 (mining under property without support rights).

242. *See Lucas*, 505 U.S. at 1035 (Kennedy, J., concurring) ("Coastal property may present such unique concerns for a fragile land system that the State can go further in regulating its development and use than the common law of nuisance might otherwise permit.").

243. Justice Scalia has suggested that this is the proper modern translation of "noxious use." *Lucas*, 505 U.S. at 1023–24. His point, of course, is that the "noxious use" formula is outmoded and should be abandoned in favor of an exception limited to actions against what would be nuisances at common law.

some plausible public justification. Justice Scalia's opinion in *Lucas* expresses skepticism about the coherency of the categories of benefit and harm. But whatever the conceptual difficulties of distinguishing regulatory purposes as benefit-conferring or harm-preventing, courts and commentators alike seem incapable of *not* talking and thinking in such terms, and the practice will almost surely continue.[244]

In the end, what constitutes a noxious use probably must be determined as a matter of social convention rather than immutable logic. The judicial conclusion in contested cases will necessarily turn on common understandings of what constitutes a "normal" use of property.[245] A regulation that prohibits a non-normal use will tend to be classified as

---

244. Indeed, even Justice Scalia in *Lucas*, while criticizing the harm/benefit distinction, employed the rhetoric of benefit creation in justifying a total wipeout categorical rule. *See Lucas*, 505 U.S. at 1018 (arguing that regulations depriving owner of all economic value "carry with them a heightened risk that private property is being pressed into some form of public service under the guise of mitigating serious public harm"); *see also* David Dana, *Natural Preservation and the Race to Develop*, 143 U. PA. L. REV. 655, 665–66 (1995) (analyzing *Lucas* and its possible implications).

245. *See* WILLIAM A. FISCHEL, REGULATORY TAKINGS: LAW, ECONOMICS, AND POLITICS 351–55 (1995) (explicating the harm/benefit distinction in terms of a normal behavior baseline); Robert C. Ellickson, *Alternatives to Zoning: Covenants, Nuisance Rules, and Fines as Land Use Controls*, 40 U. CHI. L. REV. 681, 728–33 (1973) (advancing a similar argument); *cf.* Eric T. Freyfogle, *Regulatory Takings, Methodically*, 31 ENVTL. L. REP. 10313 (2001) (urging courts to consider in takings cases whether land use restrictions are "part of the ongoing updating of ownership norms").

one that seeks to prevent a harm; a regulation that prohibits a normal use will tend to be classified as one that seeks to confer a benefit. And the common understanding of what constitutes a normal use will vary over time and from place to place. Thus, for example, whether a statute that prohibits the filling of wetlands is benefit-conferring or harm-preventing will depend on whether the filling of wetlands is perceived as normal behavior, and this perception will evolve over time as society's valuation of the different uses of wetlands changes and our understanding of the ecological functions of wetlands improves.[246] This historical and social contingency underlying the concept of noxious use means that here, as in the case of the other factors, precision remains highly elusive.

5.　*Average Reciprocity of Advantage*

Another factor mentioned in *Pennsylvania Coal* is whether the regulation secures an average reciprocity of advantage among property owners. Although this factor was omitted in *Penn Central*'s statement of relevant considerations, both the Court's opinion in *Penn Central* and subsequent case law suggest that this continues to be a relevant factor.[247] In

246. *Compare* Just v. Marinette County, 201 N.W.2d 761 (Wis.1972) (holding that ordinance prohibiting filling of wetlands falls within the police power), *with* Loveladies Harbor, Inc. v. United States, 28 F.3d 1171 (Fed.Cir.1994) (holding that wetlands regulation was a total taking under *Lucas* and that regulation did not track the common law of nuisance).

247. *See Penn Central*, 438 U.S. at 134; *see also Keystone Bituminous Coal*, 480 U.S. 470, 488, 491 (referring with approval

Lucas, Justice Scalia questioned whether the generality of a regulation should be deemed relevant in a takings—as opposed to an Equal Protection Clause—challenge.[248] But as a positive or descriptive matter, it seems that, however amorphously, the generality of regulatory burdens does weigh in the mix of judicial evaluations of takings challenges. Certainly, all others things being equal, the more general the application of a regulation—the more people, the more parcels or interests that are affected—the less likely a court is to find a taking, and, of course, vice versa.

Moreover, average reciprocity of advantage—understood to mean that the owner has not been singled out for adverse treatment, but instead is simply being required to abide by a reasonably general requirement of widespread applicability—would appear to be a good proxy for distinguishing between conventional situations covered by eminent domain as opposed to the police power. Eminent domain often applies to a single parcel of property and, even if larger numbers of owners are affected, the adjudication always proceeds parcel-by-parcel; police regulations, in contrast, usually proceed by

to "average reciprocity of advantage"); Hodel v. Irving, 481 U.S. 704, 715 (1987) (acknowledging that statute invalidated as a taking secured "something of an 'average reciprocity of advantage'" and that this weighed "weakly" in its favor); Agins v. Tiburon, 447 U.S. 255, 262 (1980) (emphasizing that the challenged ordinance limiting development of property to single-family residences would "benefit the appellants as well as the public").

248. 505 U.S. at 1027 n.14.

announcing general rules of uniform and fairly widespread applicability.

Average reciprocity, like many of the other factors, is open to multiple interpretations. One uncertainty is whether the factor applies when a regulation affects multiple owners and *all* owners are, in some degree, made better off than they would be without the regulation, or alternatively, whether it applies only when a regulation affects multiple owners and *most* (or perhaps just a *majority*) are better off than they would be without the regulation. The former interpretation, requiring universal benefit, has been endorsed by Richard Epstein.[249] He reads average reciprocity of advantage to mean that every owner must receive "implicit in-kind compensation" from the law, in the sense that their property has a higher value after the regulation than it did before. An example might be a rule requiring that all owners in a subdivision maintain a sidewalk in front of their property, which provides a continuous path for pedestrians and, in so doing, raises everyone's property values. The more relaxed interpretation would not insist on universal benefit, but simply require that the regulation be general and that most (or perhaps just a majority) property owners benefit. An example might be a rule limiting each lot in a subdivision to residential use, which might increase the value of most lots but not those located at intersections where commercial buildings could be built.

249. *See* RICHARD A. EPSTEIN, TAKINGS: PRIVATE PROPERTY AND THE POWER OF EMINENT DOMAIN 195–215 (1985).

If we view this factor, like the others, as a proxy for identifying government action along a continuum from eminent domain to police power, the more relaxed interpretation is probably sufficient. Police regulations have long included measures that benefit a majority, but not all, members of the political community. But the decided cases offer no clarification of this point.

Even if we embrace the more relaxed interpretation of average reciprocity of advantage, whether a regulation is sufficiently general to satisfy this factor will often be in the eyes of the beholder. In *Penn Central*, for example, the property owner and the dissenting Justices argued with some plausibility that owners whose buildings are singled out for landmark status are subject to especially onerous burdens not shared with most other property owners, and that this cuts in favor of finding that a preservation ordinance is a taking. But the majority responded that the landmark designation was neither so narrow in application or standardless in criteria as to suggest some form of troublesome singling out: The "New York City law applies to vast numbers of structures in the city in addition to the Terminal—all the structures contained in the 31 historic districts and over 400 individual landmarks, many of which are close to the Terminal."[250] The majority also argued that "the preservation of landmarks benefits all New York citizens and all structures, both economically and by improving the

250. *Penn Central*, 438 U.S. at 134.

quality of life in the city as a whole."[251]

Similarly, a dialogue between Justice Kennedy and Justice Stevens in *Lucas* is instructive as to how easy it is to develop opposing characterizations of the evenhandedness of government regulation. Recall that in *Lucas*, the landowner was prohibited from building on two vacant beachfront lots. Justice Kennedy stressed that others on the beach had been allowed to build and keep their houses, suggesting that Lucas had been unfairly singled out for unique burdens. Justice Stevens, however, emphasized that no one was allowed to build a new house even if it replaced an old one destroyed in a storm, and that existing homeowners on the beach were subject to an array of restrictions and requirements designed to help preserve the dunes.[252] From this perspective, the restrictions of which Lucas complained appear as part of a more general package of restrictions of wider impact.

6. *Investment-backed Expectations*

Penn Central's most important innovation was its suggestion that "the extent to which the regulation has interfered with distinct investment-backed expectations" is relevant in assessing whether a taking has occurred. The phrase "investment-backed expectations" had not previously appeared in the case law and was borrowed from Frank Michel-

251. *Id.*

252. *Compare* 505 U.S. at 1034 (Kennedy, J., concurring) *with id.* at 1074–75 (Stevens, J., dissenting).

man's law review article.[253] In *Kaiser Aetna*, one year later, the Court reformulated this factor as "reasonable investment-backed expectations."[254] Whether the formulation is "distinct expectations" or (as is more often employed today) "reasonable expectations," it is clear that the degree to which the government action reflects a sharp and unanticipated change in the permissible uses of property is today a recognized element in *ad hoc* takings analysis.

The focus on whether legal change frustrates expectations is the most difficult factor to explain in terms of proxies that distinguish between exercises of eminent domain and the police power. The government can frustrate investment-backed expectations in all sorts of ways through conventional exercises of the powers of taxation and regulation, as by changing the tax code, adopting new forms of civil liability, or imposing trade restrictions. Thus, focusing on whether government action frustrates investment-backed expectations does not directly differentiate situations in which the government should proceed by eminent domain rather than by the police power. Indeed, the focus on frustrated expectations arguably injects into takings analysis considerations more appropriate to a substantive due process analysis, which has always looked with

253. *See* Frank I. Michelman, *Property Utility, and Fairness: Comments on the Ethical Foundations of "Just Compensation" Law*, 80 HARV. L. REV. 1165, 1213 (1967). Michelman's article is discussed *supra* Chapter IIIB.

254. 444 U.S. 164, 175 (1979).

disfavor on retroactive lawmaking.[255]

One can argue, however, that the investment-backed expectations factor is at least indirectly relevant to the task of differentiating situations in which the government should proceed by eminent domain rather than by police regulation. Police regulations ordinarily apply prospectively only, that is, they govern transactions, accidents, and other events that occur in the future rather than in the past. At one time, it was assumed that police power measures could apply only in the future.[256] Today, this understanding has been relaxed, but courts still scrutinize retroactive laws more closely as a matter of due process law and apply a rule of construction that favors interpreting ambiguous regulatory laws as applying only prospectively.[257] Thus, insofar as the investment-backed expectations factor suggests that retroactive changes in permitted uses of property are less likely to be legitimate exercises of the police power, this factor can also be seen as a filter

255. *See, e.g.*, United States v. Carlton, 512 U.S. 26, 31 (1994) (holding as a matter of substantive due process law that retroactive tax legislation has a higher burden of justification than prospective legislation); Usery v. Turner Elkhorn Mining Co., 428 U.S. 1, 16–18 (1976) (holding similarly with respect to retroactive legislation adopting a new form of civil liability).

256. *See* Arizona Grocery Co. v. Atchison, T. & S.F. Ry. Co., 284 U.S. 370 (1932) (holding that agency exercising delegated authority from Congress has no authority to make retroactive changes in legislative rules it has previously adopted).

257. For due process, *see supra* note 255; for the rule of construction, *see* Landgraf v. USI Film Prod., 511 U.S. 244 (1994).

that helps to sort government actions into the categories of eminent domain versus police power.

What exactly is a reasonable (or distinct) investment-backed expectation? The Court has never defined the phrase with any greater specificity. Nevertheless, the cases are at least suggestive of some implicit criteria for how we can identify a reasonable investment-backed expectation when we see one.

First, although *Penn Central* does not cite state zoning law, the Court's analysis in many respects parallels what state courts have held in addressing challenges to zoning laws that fail to protect nonconforming uses. In general, the state courts have construed state law (statutory and constitutional) as permitting building restrictions where the owner has not yet actually begun to build—where, in *Penn Central*'s terms, expectations have not been backed up with investment, at least direct building investment. At some point in the approval and construction process, owners secure what, under state law, are called "vested rights" to build; once past this point, owners are entitled to compensation if permission is withdrawn.[258] In emphasizing that the Penn Central Company had not yet begun building

258. *See* Daniel R. Mandelker, *Entitlement to Substantive Due Process: Old Versus New Property in Land Use Litigation,* 3 WASH. U. J. L. & POL'Y 61, 76 n. 70–72 (2000) (discussing vested rights doctrine, and its close relation to equitable estoppel). For an older Supreme Court decision holding that a zoning ordinance that fails to protect nonconforming uses violates substantive due process, *see* Nectow v. City of Cambridge, 277 U.S. 183 (1928).

before permission to do so was denied, the Court implicitly invoked this nonconforming use line of state authority.

Second, recent cases such as *Lucas* and *Palazzolo v. Rhode Island*[259] suggest that historical understandings are relevant. Property owners can or should be able to rely on longstanding provisions of state law that are sufficiently prominent that they may be said to qualify the title to the owner's property. In particular, those decisions suggest that when an owner acquires property at a time when it is settled that certain uses are clearly prohibited by the law, this qualifies the owner's claim to compensation if such prohibitions are later enforced. By parity of reasoning, an owner who acquires property when it is settled that certain uses are specifically permitted by law should have a stronger claim to compensation if such uses are subsequently prohibited. In this sense, the investment-backed expectations inquiry incorporates the more general presumption against retroactive lawmaking noted above, understood here to mean legislation that eliminates a use of property that was specifically permitted at the time the property was acquired.

Third, the Court has suggested that specific individualized assurances that a certain use is permitted can help establish the reasonableness of the expectation. Thus, although there is substantial authority for the proposition that citizens follow ver-

259. 533 U.S. 606 (2001). *See supra* Chapter VB. (discussing *Lucas* and *Palazzolo*).

bal or even written guidance by government officials at their own risk,[260] assurances by government officials, while not dispositive, have been held to be relevant to investment-backed expectations.[261] It is also relevant if the formal law—statutes, regulations, etc.—specifically permit a particular use of the property at issue, as opposed to being silent on the question.[262] The visibility and magnitude of the property owner's investment also matters, with greater visibility and magnitude weighing in favor of the distinctness and reasonableness of the expectations.[263]

260. The classic case is Federal Crop Ins. Corp. v. Merrill, 332 U.S. 380 (1947) (denying crop insurance coverage to farmer who relied on oral advice of Agriculture Department official conflicting with published regulations).

261. *See* Kaiser Aetna v. United States, 444 U.S. 164, 175 (1979).

262. *See* Ruckelshaus v. Monsanto, 467 U.S. 986, 1005–14 (1984).

263. *Kaiser Aetna*, 444 U.S. at 179–80. This is generally the case in the common law of equitable estoppel, a doctrine that seems to inform, implicitly, the reasonable expectations prong of the *Penn Central* test. For example, under the common law of easements by estoppel, a property owner is more likely to be deemed to be estopped from revoking a license of access to her property if the licensee openly has made irreversible investments in reliance on the license. *See, e.g.*, Holbrook v. Taylor, 532 S.W.2d 763 (Ky.1976); *see also* RESTATEMENT OF THE LAW, THIRD, PROPERTY (SERVITUDES) § 2.10 ("the owner or occupier of land is estopped to deny the existence of a servitude burdening the land when ... the owner or occupier permitted another to use that land under circumstances in which it was reasonable to foresee that the user would substantially change position believing that the permission would not be revoked, and the user did substantially change position in reasonable reliance on that belief").

Although the foregoing criteria can be discerned in the Court's decisions, investment-backed expectations nevertheless play a very uneven role in the decided cases. The problem has not been so much one of identifying what constitutes a reasonable investment-backed expectation—although, clearly, this too could become an issue. Rather, it is that the factor fades in and out of the Court's decisions, for reasons that remain unstated and largely inexplicable.

Sometimes expectations loom very large, and become the overriding factor in the analysis. For example, in *Ruckelshaus v. Monsanto Co.*,[264] the Court resolved a takings challenge to regulations requiring disclosure of trade secret information almost exclusively in terms of the expectations of regulated firms. At times when firms had an expectation of nondisclosure, the regulation was declared to be a taking; at times when they had no such expectation, it was not. Similarly, in *Eastern Enterprises v. Apfel*,[265] the plurality opinion, although purporting to apply the three *Penn Central* factors, effectively put all its eggs in the expectations basket in holding that the imposition on a firm of a retroactive liability for increased retirement benefits for former employees was a taking.

In other cases, however, the Court has given investment-backed expectations virtually no weight at all. For example, in *Andrus v. Allard*,[266] the

264. 467 U.S. 986 (1984).

265. 524 U.S. 498 (1998).

266. 444 U.S. 51, 66–68 (1979).

Court largely ignored the expectations factor in holding that sweeping restrictions on the sale or transfer of eagle feathers and other eagle parts were not a taking. The Court seemed to acknowledge that the property in question had been acquired with a reasonable expectation that it could be used in commerce, but gave this no weight in its analysis. Similarly (although to the opposite effect), *Palazzolo*, in holding that a firm could mount an *ad hoc* takings challenge to regulations that were in effect at the time it acquired property, suggests that reasonable investment-backed expectations do not weigh very heavily in the *ad hoc* calculus. After all, where a regulation specifically prohibiting a use is in place before title is acquired, it is very hard to see how the title acquirer can have any substantial expectation—reasonable or unreasonable, distinct or indistinct—that the use will be permitted.

We close our review of the *ad hoc* factors with a cautionary note. By identifying and dissecting six factors that the Court has relied upon in resolving regulatory takings cases, we risk conveying an impression of more precision in the law than actually exists. The statement in *Pennsylvania Coal* that the cases "cannot be disposed of by general propositions" and the statement in *Penn Central* that the takings question reduces to a series of "essentially *ad hoc*, factual inquiries" capture the reality better than our attempt at classification and explanation. When a regulation goes "too far" and becomes a taking will remain, at least in contested cases, highly uncertain, and is likely to remain so for some time to come.

C. A Note on Public Utility Regulation

There is another corner of takings law that appears to be governed by an *ad hoc* standard—that which applies to public utility rate orders. Public utilities are privately owned companies that, by law, must provide basic services such as electricity, natural gas, telephony, and common carrier transportation to the public. Often such companies are natural or legal monopolies (or both). Public utilities generally have their rates set by federal or state agencies, and the Supreme Court has held that the Takings Clause requires that these rates provide utilities a reasonable, non-confiscatory rate of return on their investment.[267] No set formula is required to be used by regulatory agencies in setting public utility rates, and their factual determinations receive substantial deference by reviewing courts.

In assessing takings challenges to public utility rate orders, the Court has applied an *ad hoc* standard that focuses on different factors than those associated with the *ad hoc* approach of *Pennsylvania Coal* and *Penn Central*. The factors that are relied upon in the usual regulatory takings context—diminution in value, the character of the government action, and so forth—appear to play no

267. *See* Duquesne Light Co. v. Barasch, 488 U.S. 299 (1989); FPC v. Hope Natural Gas Co., 320 U.S. 591 (1944).

role in this area. Instead, the Court has said that courts should determine the total effect on the utility of all aspects of a rate order, and consider such factors as whether the order affords a rate of return commensurate with investments of comparable risk, whether it permits the utility to raise additional capital, and whether it reflects a fair balancing of investor and consumer interests.[268]

There is, however, another way to read the public utility cases, which has some warrant in the history of regulation of public utility rates.[269] On this view, the public utility cases are in fact subject to a categorical takings rule, which says that public utility property is "taken" once it is dedicated to public service. Public utility companies, by reason of common-carrier or universal service obligations, typically may not exit their service area without regulatory permission, and while they continue to serve have no choice but to supply services on a nondiscriminatory basis to any person who requests them. In effect, public utility property has been conscripted into a public use, as much as if the government had condemned the property and directed it to the same public use itself. Under this alternative understanding, the *ad hoc* balancing that occurs in the public utility cases is designed not to identify

268. *See Duquesne*, 488 U.S. at 310 (return on investments of comparable risk); *id.* at 312 (ability to raise capital); *Hope*, 320 U.S. at 603 (balancing of investor and consumer interests).

269. *See* John N. Drobak, *From Turnpike to Nuclear Power: The Constitutional Limits on Utility Rate Regulation*, 65 B.U. L. REV. 65, 70–81 (1985); Thomas W. Merrill, *Constitutional Limits on Physician Price Controls*, 21 HASTINGS CONST. L.Q. 635, 639–50 (1994).

whether there has been a taking—that is established by the duty to serve the public—but rather whether the regulatory agency has adopted an order that provides "just compensation" to the utility.

This alternative theory has interesting implications for the hotly-debated question whether the public utility standard applies not only to rate orders but also when the government opens what was formerly a monopoly service area to competition, as has occurred in long-distance telephone service and, in part, local telephone and electricity service.[270] As long as the incumbent utility continues to be subject to a legal duty to act as the provider of last resort—meaning it cannot exit the service area and must provide service to anyone who requests it— then its property would continue to be deemed to have been taken under the categorical rule. Thus, deregulation orders that open service areas to competition, no less than rate orders, would be subject to scrutiny under the public utility standard to assure that competition does not deprive the incumbent utility of a reasonable rate of return.

Entities subject to rate or price controls—or deregulatory competition—will generally find it more helpful to invoke the public utility takings standard than the generic takings rules of *Lucas* and *Penn*

270. For extended discussions of this issue, *see* J. GREGORY SIDAK & DANIEL F. SPULBER, DEREGULATORY TAKINGS AND THE REGULATORY CONTRACT (1997); William J. Baumol & Thomas W. Merrill, *Deregulatory Takings, Breach of the Regulatory Contract, and the Telecommunications Act of 1996*, 72 N.Y.U. L. REV. 1037 (1997); Herbert Hovenkamp, *The Takings Clause and Improvident Regulatory Bargains*, 108 YALE L.J. 801 (1999); Susan Rose–Ackerman & Jim Rossi, *Disentangling Deregulatory Takings*, 86 VA. L. REV. 1435 (2000).

Central. The public utility cases do not require an entity to show that its enterprise has been rendered totally valueless or even that it has suffered a severe diminution in the value of its property. The entity need only show a rate of return that is "inadequate to compensate equity holders for the risk associated with their investments."[271]

There are, however, some potential pitfalls associated with the public utility line of authority. These cases do not necessarily guarantee full compensation, but rather only reasonable compensation, judged with a good deal of deference on factual matters to regulators.[272] And in availing itself of the public utility line of authority, an entity must concede that it knowingly operates in an environment of intensive government regulation. The Court has on occasion suggested that entities that operate in such an environment necessarily have reduced expectations of regulatory constancy, which may qualify their ability to challenge policy changes under a variety of legal theories.[273]

271. *Duquesne*, 488 U.S. at 312.

272. It is, of course, difficult to say what full compensation means in the context of regulated utilities, as they do not operate in a thick and relatively free market. The point is simply that a court could more readily justify a modest compensation award under *Duquesne* than under standard just compensation precedents. For a justification of judicial deference in public utility takings cases, *see* Richard J. Pierce, Jr., *Public Utility Regulatory Takings: Should the Judiciary Attempt to Police the Political Institutions?*, 77 GEO. L.J. 2031 (1989).

273. *See, e.g.*, Energy Reserves Group v. Kansas Power & Light Co., 459 U.S. 400 (1983) (arguing that companies operating in heavily regulated environment have a reduced expectation that the state will not seek to impair their contracts); Exxon Corp. v. Eagerton, 462 U.S. 176, 194 (1983) (rejecting Contract Clause challenge to changes governing heavily regulated oil and gas industry despite its recognition that the changes had restricted contractual obligations). *See also* Robert A. Graham, *The Constitution, the Legislature, and Unfair Surprise: Toward a Reliance–Based Approach to the Contract Clause*, 92 MICH. L. REV. 398, 416 (1993) ("laws touching upon the subject matter of the statute in a state or even another jurisdiction might create heavy regulation. Whether this also means that tangential regulation might render an entire industry heavily regulated is not clear.").

Chapter VII

Just Compensation

The most frequently litigated question under the Takings Clause involves the measure of "just compensation." This is because traditional eminent domain proceedings far outnumber regulatory takings cases, and in most eminent domain proceedings, the only contested issue is the amount of compensation. Given that questions about the measure of compensation arise with some frequency, there is a large body of judicial precedent that addresses the meaning of just compensation. We make no attempt to summarize all of this law here, but will concentrate on a few of the more fundamental issues.

A. The Fair Market Value Standard

The basic legal standard for determining what constitutes just compensation is well established: the owner is entitled to the fair market value of the property taken by the condemning authority. Fair market value, in turn, refers to the amount that a willing buyer would pay a willing seller of the property, taking into account all possible uses to which the property might be put other than the use contemplated by the taker.[274]

All of this sounds straightforward, and would be, if takings took place in thick markets in which there were many buyers and sellers. But, as we saw in Chapter III, eminent domain is used almost exclusively in thin markets, where there is usually only one seller who has a monopoly over some resource needed for a public project. Takings involve forced exchanges of unique property rights, typically rights in land, in circumstances where voluntary exchange has failed. So the fair market value standard is inherently problematic. How do courts determine the "fair market value" of an asset for which there is no readily identifiable market price?

The answer is that fair market value is determined using a variety of valuation techniques that are familiar to anyone who has been involved in the appraisal of real estate, whether it be for purposes of establishing tax values, estate planning, or in listing property for sale. The four most common techniques are: (1) examination of recent sales prices for the property in question; (2) examination of recent sales prices for other properties in the area deemed to be comparable to the property in question; (3) capitalization of the actual or potential rental value of the property in question; and (4) calculation of the cost of rebuilding the property minus depreciation to reflect its age and wear and

274. United States v. Miller, 317 U.S. 369, 374 (1943); 4 PHILIP NICHOLS, NICHOLS' THE LAW OF EMINENT DOMAIN § 12.02[1] (Julius L. Sackman ed., 3d ed. 1964).

tear.[275] Different jurisdictions have different rules about which techniques are most preferred, and often the determination of which type of benchmark to use is left to the discretion of the court, depending on the circumstances of the case.

What actually happens in a case in which there is a dispute about the measure of compensation? Basically, the condemning authority introduces evidence, often through the testimony of expert witnesses, which follows one or more of the accepted valuation techniques, and tends to show that the property has a low value. The owner then introduces evidence, often using rival expert witnesses, which follows one or more of these techniques and tends to show that the property has a high value. The trier of fact, which may be a jury, will then have to determine which evidence is most persuasive. Sometimes it will accept the valuation submitted by one party or the other; often, it will reach a compromise between the positions of the two parties. The number picked by the trier of fact is deemed to be the "fair market value" of the property, and this then becomes the measure of just compensation which the taker must pay to the owner, along with interest from the date of the taking.

In public utility cases, a variation on the fair market value standard is used—the fair return on investment standard. Conceptually, the fair return

275. NICHOLS, *supra* note 274, § 12.02[1]; 1 LEWIS ORGEL, VALUATION UNDER THE LAW OF EMINENT DOMAIN §§ 136–138, 176 (2d ed. 1953); 2 ORGEL, *supra*, §§ 188–189.

standard operates in a manner similar to the fair market value standard: The objective is to determine just compensation based on benchmarks that reflect the behavior of other actors in the relevant market. Thus, in the public utility cases, one key benchmark is the rate of return on investment that investors expect to receive before committing funds to investments having risks commensurate with those of the regulated utility.[276] The regulatory agency or the court estimates the return on investment that would be generated by a proposed rate schedule, and compares this to the return on comparable investments. If the rate of return under the proposed schedule falls too far below the benchmark rate of return, the Takings Clause requires that the regulatory agency provide a rate increase or otherwise eliminate the gap in order to avoid an unconstitutional outcome. In practice, courts give regulatory agencies broad discretion in determining what constitutes a fair return on public utility investment. But the constitutional standard lurks in the background and has played an important role in structuring the inquiry that occurs in public utility rate cases.

Fair market value or fair rate of return is not the only standard that could be adopted to implement the just compensation requirement. One alternative would be to set compensation equal to the benefit received by the taker from acquiring the property.

---

276. *See* Duquesne Light Co. v. Barasch, 488 U.S. 299, 314 (1989) (stating that "[o]ne of the elements always relevant to setting the rate ... is the return investors expect given the risk of the enterprise").

This "restitution" standard would generally result in higher awards of compensation than the fair market value standard. This is because eminent domain typically increases the value of the property taken. The taking is often part of a project to assemble many contiguous parcels of land, which have a higher unit value after assembly than they did before.[277] Alternatively, the property may have some other strategic value that makes it especially valuable to the taker. Under established rules for determining just compensation, however, "It is the owner's loss, not the taker's gain, which is the measure of the value of the property taken."[278] Thus, the increment in value created by the taking itself goes to the taker rather than the owner.

Another alternative to fair market value would be to set compensation based on the loss to the owner. This "indemnification" standard would also generally result in higher awards of compensation relative to fair market value.[279] There are numerous reasons why owners may subjectively value their property more than the market does, ranging from

277. *See* Thomas W. Merrill, *The Economics of Public Use*, 72 CORNELL L. REV. 61, 98 (1986) (table summarizing the reasons why condemning authorities use eminent domain, with land assembly being the most common).

278. United States v. Causby, 328 U.S. 256, 261 (1946).

279. Language in some decisions suggests an indemnification standard. *See, e.g.*, United States v. Reynolds, 397 U.S. 14, 16 (1970) ("The owner is to be put in the same position monetarily as he would have occupied if his property had not been taken."). But there is no indication that the Court, in making these statements, was qualifying or repudiating the fair market value standard.

psychological attachment, to features of the property that have been customized to the owner's tastes, to nontransferable benefits associated with the location, to a desire to avoid the hassles of moving. Another way to make the point is to observe that if, for some reason, an owner values the property at less than its fair market value, the owner will generally sell it.

> [F]air market value is not the value that every owner of property attaches to his property but merely the value that the marginal owner attaches to *his* property. Many owners are "inframarginal" meaning that because of relocation costs, sentimental attachments, or the special suitability of the property for their particular (perhaps idiosyncratic) needs, they value their property at more than its market value (i.e., it is not "for sale").[280]

A standard of indemnification presumably would also require compensating owners for consequential damages associated with condemnation, such as lost business good will associated with the location of the property, moving expenses, and attorneys' fees. These sorts of damages are also excluded under the fair market value standard.[281] An indemnification standard would result in a lower award than fair market value only in those cases where an owner

280. Coniston Corp. v. Village of Hoffman Estates, 844 F.2d 461, 464 (7th Cir.1988) (Posner, J.).

281. *See, e.g.,* United States v. Petty Motor Co., 327 U.S. 372, 377–78 (1946). As noted below, some types of consequential damages result in compensation in partial takings cases.

obtains some offsetting benefit from the taking, such as enhanced value to an unrelated parcel of property, which would be taken into account in determining what compensation is required in order to make the owner whole. This is the one area where the market value standard works to the advantage of the owner—offsetting benefits to the owner are also disregarded under the fair market value test.[282]

Why does the law opt for the relatively stingy fair market value standard rather than either the restitution standard or the indemnification standard? One obvious reason is that the fair market test is more objective and can be applied at a lower cost than either of the two rival standards could be. The fair market standard, as we have noted, is by no means a mechanical formula. There is no "market price" that can be observed, and hence the value must be developed using various imperfect valuation techniques. But even with all its weaknesses, the market value standard is less fraught with difficulties than either value to the taker (the restitution standard) or value to the owner (the indemnification standard) would be.

Determining the value to the taker would be difficult, because condemnation is often used for public projects, such as highways, parks, or government buildings, that have no commercial measure of value. For example, there are usually no sales of

282. *See, e.g.,* United States v. Miller, 317 U.S. 369, 376–77 (1943). As noted below, offsetting benefits are taken into account in many jurisdictions in partial taking cases.

comparable properties devoted to such uses, nor are there likely to be any rental values that can be capitalized. Determining the value to the owner would also be difficult, because owners often have reasons for their attachment to their property that are difficult to verify. If the owner of a house with a fair market value of $100,000 says he would not sell for anything less than $200,000, how do we know whether this is an honest statement of the owner's subjective attachment to the house, or a negotiating ploy designed to obtain a higher award of compensation? The market value standard thus undoubtedly conserves on administrative costs relative to either the restitution standard or the indemnification standard.

It is tempting to dismiss these savings in administrative costs as simply a preference for social utility at the expense of doing full justice to property owners. But Frank Michelman's theory of just compensation suggests that individual property owners as a class may not be disfavored by the market value standard. The reader will recall from Chapter III that Michelman explained compensation practices in terms of a trade-off between demoralization costs and settlement costs.[283] The law, Michelman suggested, will tend to reduce demoralization costs only if the settlement costs of achieving such a reduction are less than the avoided demoralization costs. As applied to the rules of just compensation, this suggests that legal rules that lower the administrative costs of fixing awards of just compensation

283. *See supra* Chapter IIIB1.

should allow the legal system to be more generous in identifying the circumstances when compensation is appropriate. In other words, if we spend fewer resources in squabbling over the size of compensation awards, we can afford to compensate more people.

From this perspective, it is not implausible that property owners as a class would willingly give up a more fine-tuned measure of compensation in return for a broader or more certain guarantee of compensation. This intuition is consistent with programs like workman's compensation, which provide for caps on damages in return for greater coverage against workplace injury, as well as the practices of the insurance industry in areas such as disability insurance, where policies typically pay benefits that fall short of full indemnity but also do not require absolute proof of disability.

Another reason why an incomplete measure of compensation such as the fair market value standard may be appropriate relates to the discussion in Chapter III about fiscal illusion.[284] As we noted there, compensation can be seen as an efficiency-enhancing rule that requires the government to internalize the costs of seizing someone's property. But we also want to provide an incentive for property owners to avoid using their property in ways that increase the costs of takings. These two objectives tend to conflict: Requiring the government fully to internalize all costs of takings would provide no incentives for property owners to behave efficiently,

284. *See supra* Chapter IIIB2.

but requiring property owners fully to internalize the costs of using their property in ways inconsistent with future government takings (*i.e.*, denying all compensation) would provide no incentive for the government to behave efficiently.

One possible solution to this dilemma is to require the government to pay partial compensation when it takes property and leave the balance of the costs on the owner. This provides an incentive for the government to consider the costs of taking property, although, of course, not a perfect one. But it also provides some incentive for property owners to avoid improvident investments that increase the costs of takings, and to minimize the consequential damages associated with takings.[285] Incomplete compensation in this sense works something like a rule of comparative negligence in tort, or like deductibles and co-payment requirements in insurance contracts. These rules, like the market value standard of just compensation, provide incentives for the claimant to take precautions to minimize the costs of events that give rise to monetary liability for someone else.

A third reason for providing incomplete compensation is to subsidize the power of eminent domain. The Constitution assumes that takings will occur in the pursuit of "public uses." Most public uses— such as the construction of highways and other

---

285. Many consequential damages associated with condemnation, such as moving expenses, are subject to the control of the owner at least in part. A rule of full indemnification would almost certainly increase these costs.

infrastructure investments, the development of parks and recreation areas, and the erection of government buildings and facilities—provide important benefits to the public. Subsidies are good when they produce benefits that exceed their costs. This describes many, if not most, of the public uses associated with exercises in eminent domain— enough so that including a measure of subsidy in the computation of just compensation may be warranted. In contrast, if eminent domain awards were based on a restitution standard or were based on an indemnification standard, the subsidy element would be reduced or would disappear altogether. This would reduce the incentive to use the power to achieve ends in the public interest.

B. Partial Takings

Many (perhaps most) takings are partial takings, that is, the taker acquires only a fraction of the owner's property and leaves the balance in the owner's hands. This will often occur, for example, when the taking is for a highway or a utility right-of-way. The standard for just compensation in partial takings differs from total takings. In a partial taking, the owner is awarded not only the fair market value of the part that is taken, but also damages for loss in value to the part that is not taken.[286] In addition, States are permitted (but not

286. *See* Bauman v. Ross, 167 U.S. 548, 598 (1897); 4A NICHOLS, *supra* note 274, § 14A.01[2].

required) to reduce the award of compensation in partial takings by taking into account offsetting benefits to the part of the property that is not taken.[287]

In effect, the compensation standard for partial takings shifts part way toward an indemnification standard. The law does not shift all the way to indemnification, since consequential damages, such as attorneys' fees, continue to be excluded in the partial taking situation. What the law does in the partial takings situation, in effect, is to compute the fair market value of what the owner has before the taking, then compute the fair market value of what the owner has after the taking, and award the owner the difference.[288] The partial takings rules can thus be seen as a variant on the fair market value approach, with the wrinkle that here one does not seek the fair market value of what is acquired by the government (the usual rule), but rather the fair market value of what is taken from the owner. This wrinkle, it must be granted, in effect shifts the rule a fair way toward an indemnification standard.

The rationale for shifting part way toward an indemnification standard in partial takings cases

287. *See* 3 NICHOLS, *supra* note 274, § 8A.03.

288. *See* United States v. 8.41 Acres of Land, 680 F.2d 388, 394 (5th Cir.1982); 1 ORGEL, *supra* note 275, § 4. Some courts do not proceed this way, but rather ask the trier of fact to find the fair market value of the interest acquired by the government, and then make adjustments for damages to the part that remains and offsetting benefits to the part that remains. But the before-and-after comparison is the "simplest and perhaps most widely used approach in severance damage determinations." Georgia–Pacific Corp. v. United States, 640 F.2d 328, 336 (Ct.Cl.1980).

has never been clearly spelled out. One possible explanation would be that courts prefer the indemnification standard, but are constrained from adopting it in the total takings case by the prospect of high administrative costs. In partial takings cases, the inquiry into consequential damages and offsetting benefits is carefully confined to damages and benefits to the part of the owner's property that remains after the taking. In contrast, if one were to engage in an analysis of consequential damages and offsetting benefits in the total takings case, it is not clear what property one would look to in undertaking this analysis. Without any clear line to demarcate the inquiry, it could mushroom into an open-ended set of arguments and counter-arguments that would magnify administrative costs several times over.

Another possible explanation is that partial takings are especially prone to unfair outcomes under the fair market value standard. Consider, for example, a partial taking that leaves the owner landlocked. This could effectively reduce the value of the residual property to zero. But there would be no compensation for this loss under a standard that awards only the fair market value of what the government has acquired. Alternatively, consider a partial taking that puts a public street through to land that was previously landlocked. Here, the taking transforms land that was previously worth very little into a valuable asset. Yet, under the fair market value standard, the government would be required to pay some compensation to the owner, even though he has already received a substantial windfall. Shifting to a rule that awards the fair market value of what is taken eliminates both of these extreme outcomes.

A final possible explanation is that partial takings, unlike total takings, interfere with the scale of the owner's unit of property, thereby generating an additional type of cost that the government needs to take into account in structuring its takings. Suppose, for example, that A owns a city lot and the government wants to take 80 percent of the lot for a new street. Under ordinary rules, the government would pay the fair market value of what it acquires—80 percent of a lot. But it is not unlikely that the 20 percent that remains after the taking will be too small to build on, and hence has been rendered largely worthless. Limiting the government to paying for the 80 percent of the lot it acquires would thus create an external cost to the owner that the government would have no incentive to take into account. The result might be that takers would have an incentive to act strategically to structure their takings as partial takings in order to leave owners with uncompensated losses.

Whatever the explanation, partial takings present an important exception to the general rule that the condemning authority pays the fair market value of the interest it acquires. In this one context, the condemning authority pays the fair market value of what the owner loses.

C. Temporary Takings

Takings can be less than total in terms of time as well as space. When the government takes property for a limited period of time, after which it restores full possession and control to the owner, this is referred to as a temporary taking. It has long been established that when the government takes property for a limited time through formal eminent domain proceedings, the usual rule applies—the government must pay just compensation for the fair market value of the interest taken.[289] In such a case, the government has in effect acquired an involuntary leasehold estate. Just compensation takes the form of a lease payment, paid either periodically or in a lump sum, based on the fair market rental value of the property taken.

For many years, it was unclear how the temporary takings analysis applied in regulatory takings cases. Regulatory takings claims entail great uncertainty, and often many years elapse between the imposition of a regulation and a final judicial determination that the regulation has effected an uncompensated taking of property. When such a final judgment is entered, the government has several options: it can withdraw the regulation, it can amend it so as to eliminate the taking, or it can exercise the power of eminent domain and take formal title to the property. But without regard to

289. *See* Kimball Laundry Co. v. United States, 338 U.S. 1 (1949); United States v. General Motors Corp., 323 U.S. 373 (1945).

how the government elects to proceed prospectively, what remedy does the owner have for the period between the imposition of the regulation and the time the taking is rectified?

Some state courts, most prominently the California Supreme Court, took the position that the owner had no remedy for the period between imposition of a regulation and a final judicial determination that the regulation has affected a taking.[290] After several false starts in seeking to review this rule, the Supreme Court eventually held in *First English Evangelical Lutheran Church v. Los Angeles County*[291] that the California approach violates the Takings Clause. The Court reasoned that the imposition of a regulation that is subsequently invalidated as a taking is a temporary taking, just as if the government had formally taken a leasehold interest in the property by eminent domain. Consequently, the state has no choice under the Constitution but to pay just compensation to the owner for the period of such temporary takings.

The decision in *First English Evangelical Lutheran Church* was premised on the understanding that the regulation in that case—which prohibited any construction of buildings on the owner's property because of a danger of flooding—deprived the owner of any use of the property and hence operated as a taking from the time the regulation was imposed. It does not follow, of course, that other regulations

290. Agins v. Tiburon, 598 P.2d 25 (Cal.1979), *aff'd on other grounds*, 447 U.S. 255 (1980).

291. 482 U.S. 304 (1987).

that interfere with the use of property for some period of time amount to a taking. The Court noted that quite different questions "would arise in the case of normal delays in obtaining building permits, changes in zoning ordinances, variances, and the like."[292] In *Tahoe–Sierra Preservation Council v. Tahoe Regional Planning Agency*,[293] the Court construed the category of government regulations that escape categorical takings treatment to include even multi-year moratoria on land development.

Here, as elsewhere, it is important to remember that the Takings Clause applies only when the government takes "private property." The regulation must therefore have the effect of transferring an interest in private property from the owner to the state, such as a leasehold estate or an easement, before it can be deemed to cause a temporary taking giving rise to a claim for money compensation.[294]

D. Takings of Property Subject to Divided or Restricted Ownership

One of the most analytically difficult issues in determining just compensation arises when the gov-

292. *Id.* at 321.

293. 122 S.Ct. 1465 (2002).

294. For example, in *Tahoe–Sierra*, both the majority and the dissenting opinions appear to acknowledge that regulations that confer the functional equivalent of a leasehold upon the government would constitute a compensable taking. The opinions, however, differ as to what constitutes the functional equivalent of a leasehold. Takings law, once again, conflates into a debate about the nature of the underlying property interests and thus, more generally, into a debate about the definition of "property."

ernment takes property where the title is divided among two or more persons or includes legal restrictions on the use of the property. The most common divided ownership issue involves landlord-tenant relations, but the issue also arises when the property taken has restrictions on use built into the title. Such restrictions can arise either through easements or servitudes, or from restrictions on use contained in a defeasible fee simple, for example where land is conveyed to a school district so long as it is used for school purposes.

The general rule in all these cases, and the starting point for sound analysis, is that the government pays the fair market value of the interest it acquires.[295] Thus, if the condemnation results in the government acquiring an undivided fee simple—the most common outcome—the government should pay for an undivided fee simple, even if the title was divided or restricted prior to the taking. Questions will arise about how the award should be divided among the different stakeholders—the landlord and the tenant, or the owner of the servient estate and owner of the easement. But the first issue is to determine the size of the total award, and here the general principle that the government pays for what it gets provides the answer.

295. The argument here generally follows Victor P. Goldberg et al., *Bargaining in the Shadow of Eminent Domain: Valuing and Apportioning Condemnation Awards Between Landlord and Tenant*, 34 UCLA L. Rev. 1083 (1987).

The traditional explanation for the rule that the government pays for what it gets is that eminent domain actions are *in rem*. The government is condemning a particular thing—a *"res"*—not the various interests that different individuals have in the thing.[296] The government must therefore pay the fair market value of the thing acquired, not the value of the various bundles of rights that have been taken from the previous owners.

This conceptual explanation is bolstered by considerations of equal treatment. Suppose the rule were the opposite—that the government must pay the value of the interests that the parties give up, rather than the value of what it acquires. Suppose further (as is often true) that divided ownership or limitations on ownership will depress the value of the sum of the individual interests below the value of an undivided interest. In these circumstances, some savvy parties would include in the lease or deed that, in the event of a condemnation, the division of ownership or the limitation on use will automatically terminate. Such a clause would insure that these owners would be able to divide an award equal to the value of an undivided fee simple. Meanwhile, other parties with identical divisions of ownership or restrictions on use would not have the foresight to include an automatic termination clause. These parties would be compensated only for the lower value of a divided or restricted parcel. The

296. This is why eminent domain actions sometimes have names such as United States v. 50 Acres of Land, 469 U.S. 24 (1984), or United States v. 564.54 Acres of Land, 441 U.S. 506 (1979). The land is literally the defendant.

result would be that otherwise similarly situated owners would receive different compensation, based solely on observance of a formality having no bearing on the substantive rights or obligations of the parties.

The rule that the government must pay for what it gets is also supported by efficiency considerations. If the government had to pay only the aggregate value of the interests that the parties give up, then the government would often pay less for taking property subject to divided ownership or use restrictions than it would have to pay for property already held as an undivided fee simple. This would create an incentive for the government to condemn land held in divided or restricted ownership. For example, the government would have an incentive to build a highway through land restricted for use as a park, rather than vacant land held in fee simple, because land restricted for use as a park would have a lower market value than otherwise identical land held as a fee simple.[297] But it is doubtful that this is the correct result from a social point of view: The park may generate important social benefits that are not reflected in its reduced market value. Making the government pay the market value of the interest it acquires helps to eliminate such potentially perverse incentives.

Once the principle that the government pays for what it gets is established, then it is necessary to

297. *Cf.* Ink v. City of Canton, 212 N.E.2d 574 (Ohio 1965) (involving condemnation of land held under a defeasible fee limiting it to use as a park).

develop rules for allocating the award among the multiple stakeholders. Whatever the rules of allocation, they should probably be regarded as default rules, subject to modification by the parties. For example, commercial leases often include "condemnation clauses" that specify how condemnation awards will be divided between landlord and tenant in the event of a taking. Since commercial leases are usually arm's length bargains between sophisticated parties represented by lawyers, there is no reason not to enforce these clauses according to their terms.[298]

The content of the default rules of allocation varies depending on the nature of the divided or restricted ownership, and for many issues that do not arise that often, the rule will not be clearly specified in many jurisdictions. If one were looking for a general principle here, perhaps it would be to give the entire award to the "residual claimant," that is, to the party who has the right to the residual value of the asset after all specific contractual allocations of value have been taken into account.[299] In the landlord-tenant context, for example, if the tenant has a month-to-month tenancy and the landlord is responsible for maintenance of the building and common areas, then the landlord typically would be the residual claimant. Conversely, if the lease is a long-term ground rent lease where the tenant supplies the building and mainte-

298. *See* Goldberg, *supra* note 295, at 1090–92.

299. On the concept of residual claimancy, *see* YORAM BARZEL, ECONOMIC ANALYSIS OF PROPERTY RIGHTS 38–39 (2d ed. 1997).

nance, then the tenant typically would be the residual claimant. For most use restrictions, whether imposed by servitude or by defeasible fee, the party in possession of the premises would be the residual claimant. Such all-or-nothing default rules would eliminate costly disputes over valuation that can arise when awards must be split between two or more claimants. They would, of course, be subject to modification by advance agreement of the parties if they had some specific reason for wanting a more fine-tuned allocation of condemnation awards.

CHAPTER VIII

PUBLIC USE

The Takings Clause says that just compensation must be paid when private property is taken "for public use." The Supreme Court has interpreted these words to mean that takings of private property are constitutional only if just compensation is paid *and* the taking is for a public use. Thus, an exercise of the power of eminent domain for which full and adequate compensation is given will nevertheless be struck down as unconstitutional if the taking is for a private, rather than a public, use.

Although in theory the public use limitation could be a significant barrier to takings of property, in practice it has proven to be rather toothless. The Supreme Court has indicated that great deference should be given to legislative determinations of what constitutes a public use: "[W]here the exercise of the eminent domain power is rationally related to a conceivable public purpose, the Court has never held a compensated taking to be proscribed by the Public Use Clause."[300] Courts, in fact, have upheld a variety of takings followed by transfers to nongovernmental entities against the claim that this violates the public use requirement.

300. Hawaii Hous. Auth. v. Midkiff, 467 U.S. 229, 241 (1984).

For example, in the notorious *Poletown* case, the Michigan Supreme Court approved the plan of the City of Detroit to condemn 465 acres of land that included residences, churches, and storefront shops, and reconvey it on favorable terms to the General Motors Corporation for the construction of a new automobile assembly plant.[301] The public use identified by the court as supporting this exercise of the taking power included the creation of jobs, preservation of tax revenues, and avoiding the social deterioration caused by a declining industrial and population base.[302] Other courts have upheld takings condemning landlords' reversions to reconvey them to tenants as part of a "land reform" program, and takings condemning a sports franchise to keep a professional football team from relocating to another city.[303]

A. The Deferential Approach to Public Use

The courts' generally deferential attitude may rest in part on uncertainty about the exact significance of the phrase "for public use" in the Takings Clause. In contrast to the other three linguistic elements of the Clause (private property, taking, and just compensation), the words "for public use" do not necessarily operate grammatically as a limitation on governmental power. The words modify

301. Poletown Neighborhood Council v. City of Detroit, 304 N.W.2d 455 (Mich.1981).

302. *Id.* at 467.

303. *See* Hawaii Hous. Auth. v. Midkiff, 467 U.S. 229 (1984) (land reform); City of Oakland v. Oakland Raiders, 646 P.2d 835 (Cal.1982) (sports franchise).

"taken" and thus clearly establish that the Clause is about a subset of takings—those for public use— as opposed to all possible types of takings. But this narrowing language could mean one of three things.

First, the language could mean that the Framers were simply describing the type of taking for which just compensation must be given—a taking for public use. On this reading, the words "for public use" were intended as a synonym for the exercise of the power of eminent domain.[304] If this interpretation were accepted, then the public use language would serve to limit the Takings Clause to exercises of the power of eminent domain, as opposed to other types of power, such as the police power.

Second, the language could mean that compensation must be paid if property is taken for public use, but not if it is taken for a private use. This reading was urged by some lawyers in the early Nineteenth Century, and has been revived by some modern commentators.[305] On this interpretation, the gov-

304. As observed in one Nineteenth Century treatise:

If the intent had been to make the words, *public use*, a limitation, the natural form of expression would have been: "Private property shall not be taken *except* for public use, nor without just compensation." It is certainly questionable whether anything more was intended by the provision in question than as though it read: "Private property shall not be taken *under the power of eminent domain* without just compensation."

JOHN LEWIS, A TREATISE ON THE LAW OF EMINENT DOMAIN ii (1st ed. 1888).

305. *See* MORTON HORWITZ, THE TRANSFORMATION OF AMERICAN LAW, 1780–1860, at 65 (1977); Roger Clegg, *Reclaiming the Text*

ernment could freely engage in uncompensated expropriations of private property for *private use*—at least the Takings Clause (as opposed to the Due Process or Equal Protection Clauses) would impose no barrier to such action.

From the Nineteenth Century on, courts have rejected each of the foregoing interpretations of the public use language, and instead have adopted a third construction: that property may be taken only if the taking is for a public, rather than a private, use. The reason courts found this reading congenial is not hard to identify. From the time of the framing of the Constitution onward, private takings, that is, takings of property from A to give it to B, have been regarded as the essence of unjust government action.[306] Given even a modest degree of interpretational leeway, which the Takings Clause surely provides on this point, courts and commentators have agreed that the public use language is designed to preclude purely private takings.[307]

*of the Takings Clause,*46 S.C. L. Rev. 531 (1995); Jed Rubenfeld, *Usings*, 102 YALE L.J. 1077 (1993).

306. *See, e.g.*, Calder v. Bull, 3 U.S. (3 Dall.) 386, 388 (1798) (opinion of Chase, J.) (stating that "a law that takes property from A. and gives it to B." would be "contrary to the great first principles of the social compact"); *see generally* John V. Orth, *Taking From A and Giving To B: Substantive Due Process and the Case of the Shifting Paradigm*, 14 CONST. COMM. 337 (1997).

307. *See, e.g.*, Cole v. City of La Grange, 113 U.S. 1, 6 (1885) (opinion of Gray, J.) (stating that legislatures do not have the power to "take private property, without the owner's consent, for any but a public object"); Missouri Pac. R.R. Co. v. Nebraska, 164 U.S. 403, 417 (1896) (opinion of Gray, J.) (a private taking

Although the Court has never repudiated this understanding of the public use requirement, the history of judicial enforcement of the public use limitation, at least since the 1930s, has been one of steady erosion. This is revealed most prominently in statements about the applicable standard of review. Although the question whether a taking satisfies the public use requirement is ultimately a matter for judicial decision,[308] the Court has indicated that great deference will be given to legislative determinations as to what constitutes a public use. The Court's most recent pronouncement on the subject appears to equate the standard of review with the "rationality review" that applies to economic regulations under the Equal Protection and Due Process Clauses of the Constitution: a finding of public use will be upheld if a legislature rationally could have believed that the taking would promote a legitimate public purpose.[309]

The erosion is also evident in the judicial understanding of what "public use" means. Construed literally, "public use" might mean "used by the public." In other words, the taking must result in some asset or facility that is physically accessible to

"is not due process of law, and is a violation of the Fourteenth [Amendment]"); Lewis, *supra* note 304, at 214.

308. *See* Cincinnati v. Vester, 281 U.S. 439, 446 (1930) ("the question what is a public use is a judicial one").

309. Hawaii Hous. Auth. v. Midkiff, 467 U.S. 229, 241 (1984) ("rationally related to a conceivable public purpose"); *id.* at 242–43 ("[w]hen the legislature's purpose is legitimate and its means are not irrational" courts will not question the wisdom of a taking).

the general public. On this reading, takings of private property for courthouses and railroads would be valid public uses, but condemnations for military bases or prisons might not be, since these are generally off-limits to the public. And private retransfers for urban renewal or land reform purposes would be precluded, since they result in transfers to private parties who have the right to exclude the public. The Supreme Court rejected the use-by-the-public test as unduly restrictive in the 1920s, and most state supreme courts have followed suit.[310]

Today, nearly all courts have settled on a broader understanding that requires only that the taking yield some public benefit or advantage.[311] This reading equates public use with "public interest." Such a test, of course, opens the door to a much wider range of takings. Government facilities off-limits to the public, such as military bases and prisons, are unproblematic public uses on this reading. In addition, private retransfers may satisfy the public use requirement, so long as some public interest ratio-

310. *See, e.g.,* Rindge Co. v. Los Angeles County, 262 U.S. 700, 707 (1923) ("It is not essential that the entire community, nor even any considerable portion, should directly enjoy or participate in an improvement in order to constitute a public use."); Prince George's County v. Collington Crossroads, Inc., 339 A.2d 278, 284 (Md.1975) (holding that concept of public use is not confined to cases in which "the public must literally or physically be permitted to use the property taken by eminent domain"); *but see, e.g.,* Karesh v. City Council, 247 S.E.2d 342 (S.C.1978) (reaffirming the use-by-the-public interpretation as a matter of South Carolina constitutional law).

311. *See* Lawrence Berger, *The Public Use Requirement in Eminent Domain*, 57 OR. L. REV. 203, 205–25 (1978).

nale, such as eliminating urban blight or breaking up an "oligopolistic" land market, can be cited in support of the taking.

The Supreme Court has expressed its endorsement of this broad public interest interpretation by stating that the public use requirement is "coterminous with the scope of a sovereign's police powers."[312] This is confusing, since the distinction between the power of eminent domain and the police power is the foundation of the regulatory takings doctrine. An exercise of the power of eminent domain requires compensation; an exercise of the police power does not. If the scope of the power of eminent domain is "coterminous" with the police power, then either all exercises of the police power require compensation or all exercises of the power of eminent domain do not, neither of which, of course, is the law. What the Court appears to mean is that just as the police power may be exercised to achieve any legitimate public benefit or advantage not prohibited by the Constitution, so the power of eminent domain may be exercised to achieve any public benefit or advantage not prohibited by the Constitution.

The Court's unfortunate statement about public use being "coterminous" with the police power nevertheless provides an important clue to why courts have been so reluctant to give any teeth to the public use limitation. The coercive powers of the government can be classified under such headings

312. *Midkiff*, 467 U.S. at 240; *see also* Berman v. Parker, 348 U.S. 26, 32 (1954).

as the power of taxation, the police power, and the power of eminent domain. Once the courts stopped trying to identify any clear boundaries to the exercise of the powers of taxation and the police power after the 1930s, it made little sense to continue to impose a more restrictive limitation on the ends to which the power of eminent domain could be deployed. Indeed, eminent domain is, if anything, less intrusive than other powers, because eminent domain requires the payment of just compensation. Thus, there is an underlying logic to the courts' relaxation of the limits on the ends to which eminent domain can be deployed. The inconvenient fact that the Takings Clause includes a public use limitation, whereas the powers of taxation and regulation are not limited by any express textual provision about ends, has not prevented courts from seeking to harmonize the scope of these three powers.

B. The Need to Police the Boundary Between Coerced and Voluntary Exchange

The public use requirement has always been regarded as a limitation on the *ends* that the government may pursue using the power of eminent domain. But there is another way of looking at the problem: whether eminent domain is an appropriate *means* of pursuing any particular public purpose or objective.[313] We can distinguish among three differ-

313. *See* Thomas W. Merrill, *The Economics of Public Use*, 72 CORNELL L. REV. 61 (1986).

ent means by which the government can acquire resources. At one extreme, we have the police power: the government can acquire resources without the owner's consent and without compensation. Next we have eminent domain: the government can acquire resources without the owner's consent but must pay compensation. Finally we have the situation that would prevail if it were determined that a particular type of acquisition was permissible but beyond the power of eminent domain: the government could acquire resources only with the owner's consent, that is, only through voluntary exchange in the market.

Current takings law actively polices the boundary between the first two means—the police power and the power of eminent domain. The policing is done in the name of the regulatory takings doctrine, considered in Chapters V and VI. But the boundary between eminent domain and voluntary exchange is also important. To use the now-familiar terminology introduced by Calabresi and Melamed, this boundary marks the choice between liability rules and property rules, an important distinction that cuts across many areas of the law.[314] Unfortunately, we have no constitutional doctrine that polices this boundary—other than the public use requirement. And, as we have seen, the language and traditions surrounding the public use requirement focus exclu-

314. Guido Calabresi & A. Douglas Melamed, *Property Rules, Liability Rules, and Inalienability: One View of the Cathedral*, 85 HARV. L. REV. 1089 (1972).

sively on the legitimate ends of government action, not the choice of means to achieve those ends.

There are three general reasons why we might want to have a constitutional doctrine that polices the choice between voluntary exchange and forced exchange with compensation, that is, between property rules and liability rules. First, as detailed in Chapter VII, the formula for fixing condemnation awards undercompensates the condemnee in most situations. In a voluntary exchange, the owner presumably will not part with the property until the government offers a price that exceeds the subjective value the owner attaches to the property, and that covers all consequential damages, including relocation costs. Voluntary exchange thus guarantees full compensation. Forced exchange ignores these elements of individual value and concern, and thus necessarily introduces a degree of unfairness and inefficiency.[315]

Second, as also discussed in Chapter VII, eminent domain overcompensates or subsidizes the condemnor of the property. Subsidies are not always bad, of course. It may be entirely appropriate to use eminent domain to subsidize the production of various

315. Responding to these kinds of concerns, Margaret Jane Radin has suggested that eminent domain should be restricted when the government seeks to acquire property that implicates interests in "personhood" rather than fungible wealth. *See* Margaret Jane Radin, *Property and Personhood*, 34 STAN. L. REV. 957 (1982). But it is not clear whether this distinction could be administered very easily, given conflicting perspectives about whether to classify things like showpiece second homes and small business establishments as personal or fungible.

public goods, like roads, schoolhouses, and defense bases. But the more widely available these subsidies become, the more disadvantages they accumulate. One drawback is that the subsidies may induce competition to secure the benefits of the power of eminent domain. The resources expended in such competitions (which economists call rent-seeking) are generally regarded as wasteful. Another problem is that there may be cases in which we do not want to subsidize people who need additional property, because they have acted carelessly or even deliberately in getting themselves into a situation where additional property is needed. Better to impose sanctions in these situations, in order to deter careless or strategic behavior. A third is that subsidies may produce an inefficiently large production of the subsidized activity. If developers of shopping centers can use eminent domain to acquire land for new shopping center sites, this will subsidize the development of shopping centers and conceivably may result in too many shopping centers being built.

Each of the foregoing reasons for restricting eminent domain all relate to problems of valuation, and thus might be eliminated if we could devise a perfect method for valuing property and apportioning gains from takings that would eliminate all under- or overcompensation. But there is a third consideration that operates independently of these measurement-related problems. This is a general moral/political objection to government coercion. Eminent domain always entails the exercise of governmental power to coerce some person to give up property against his or her will. Just as property owners and their sympathizers will perceive an injustice if their property is taken by deliberate collective action without compensation,[316] so there is a perception of injustice associated with the prospect of having property taken by deliberate collective action *with* compensation. Because compensation is paid the perception of injustice surely is less. But the element of coercion remains, and many people regard any exercise of coercion as an evil to be avoided if possible in a free society. This too supports the case for some device confining the exercise of eminent domain to cases of genuine public need or necessity.

C. Alternatives to the Analysis of Ends

How then can courts police the exercise of the power of eminent domain so as to minimize problems of under- and overcompensation and unnecessary government coercion, assuming that vigorous enforcement of the "public use" requirement is ill-suited to these purposes? Commentators have offered a variety of suggestions.

One possibility, suggested by Frank Michelman's classic article, would be to have courts engage in cost-benefit analysis to assure that public benefits

316. Frank I. Michelman, *Property, Utility, and Fairness: Comments on the Ethical Foundations of "Just Compensation" Law*, 80 Harv. L. Rev. 1165, 1210–11 (1967) (arguing that people suffer a unique form of demoralization when their property is taken through intentional governmental action).

from the taking exceed the costs.[317] The benefits
would be measured by the value of the property to
the condemning authority, not just the market value to the condemnee. The costs would include not
just the costs of compensation, but also any uncompensated subjective value and any demoralization
costs associated with coerced transfer of property by
the government.

The cost-benefit proposal, however, contemplates
a role for courts for which they are ill-suited. As
discussed in Chapter VII, one reason why judicial
awards of just compensation do not seek to measure
the benefits to the condemnor or the subjective
losses and demoralization of the condemnee is that
these values are intangible and speculative, and are
not readily susceptible to judicial determination. To
impose a duty on courts to measure these values as
part of a global cost-benefit inquiry would undo the
longstanding policy reasons for restricting courts to
considering objective evidence of market value in
setting condemnation awards. Indeed, one can argue that if estimates of these speculative values
were to be developed by courts, it would be better to
use them to adjust the measure of compensation,
rather than to have courts factor them into a cost-
benefit analysis used to screen out certain exercises
in eminent domain.

A second possibility, advanced by Richard Epstein, would be to have courts review exercises of

317. *Id.* at 1241 (proposing a formula under which courts
would invalidate takings if the total costs exceed the total benefits).

eminent domain in order to determine whether they are designed to produce "public goods."[318] Public goods are things like national defense and the legal system that, once supplied, can be enjoyed by everyone, and as they are consumed, leave an undiminished amount for others to enjoy.[319] Epstein argues that if eminent domain is used to produce a public good, then all members of society will stand to benefit, and the risk of abuse of the power to transfer wealth from one person to another is greatly reduced. Where eminent domain is used to produce a non-public good, then, in order to minimize the risks of under- and overcompensation and discourage coercive transfers of property, Epstein would require that the condemnor share the surplus generated by the condemnation with the condemnee, as under some early Mill Acts that required condemnors to pay compensation equal to 150 percent of fair market value.[320]

As with the cost-benefit proposal, Epstein's public goods constraint enlists judges in a task for which they are not trained and are not likely to perform with distinction. The concept of public goods is very elastic, and can be defined either narrowly, such that only national defense and the legal system and a few other things are included, or broadly, such that any activity that generates positive externali-

318. RICHARD EPSTEIN, TAKINGS: PRIVATE PROPERTY AND THE POWER OF EMINENT DOMAIN 166–69 (1985).

319. Economists refer to these properties as "impossibility of exclusion" and "jointness in supply." *See* DENNIS MUELLER, PUBLIC CHOICE II, at 11 (1989).

320. Epstein, *supra* note 318, at 174–75.

ties is included. It is very unlikely that judges would be comfortable attempting to explicate the concept—or that they would reach consistent results if they did. The related idea that courts should award enhanced compensation when takings do not entail public goods is also problematic. Courts have always been reluctant to derive numerical standards from general principles, whether they are statutes of limitations or multipliers for punitive damages. Epstein's proposal seems very "legislative," and probably should be implemented, if at all, through legislation.

A third possibility, proposed by one of the authors,[321] is simply to insist that courts strictly enforce procedural limitations on the exercise of eminent domain. Eminent domain is a judicial proceeding that affects discrete interests in property, and as such is subject to the Due Process Clauses, as well as the Takings Clause. Thus, a property owner is entitled to notice and a fair hearing into all contested issues of fact and law before her property may be taken by condemnation.[322] These constitutional procedures are supplemented in all jurisdictions by various statutory procedures that specify how condemnations are to be conducted. As a sovereign prerogative of the legislature, eminent domain also requires the enactment of a statute authorizing the taking, or at least a statute that delegates, in a constitutional-

321. *See* Merrill, *supra* note 313, at 77–81.

322. *See* State of Washington *ex rel.* Seattle Title Trust Co. v. Roberge, 278 U.S. 116, 121 (1928).

ly permissible manner, the power to take property to some municipal government, administrative agency, or public utility. Collectively, these procedural requirements are costly; they can be described as imposing a "due process tax" on the exercise of eminent domain.

If the various hearing and delegation requirements associated with eminent domain are strictly enforced, then coercive transactions will almost always be more expensive than voluntary transactions, at least in thick markets where there are multiple buyers and sellers for the resource in question. In effect, imposition of the due process tax makes the exercise of eminent domain largely self-regulating: It will be used only where the surplus to the taker is greater than the due process tax. Judicial enforcement of the due process tax thus ensures that the use of eminent domain will at least partially track the results that would obtain if courts were capable of conducting a global cost-benefit analysis to screen out impermissible exercises of the power.

Obviously, the due process tax is a very crude instrument for confining the exercise of eminent domain in an appropriate manner. For example, if a particular taking entails very large subjective losses to the condemnee the taking may go forward, even if those losses are greater than the gain to the condemnor, provided the gain to the condemnor exceeds the due process tax. Thus, the due process tax will filter out only some of the questionable uses of eminent domain, and, indeed, will often fail to catch those cases where uncompensated costs are at their greatest.

Nevertheless, the due process tax has the virtue of imposing a partial solution to the problem, and does so by enlisting the courts in the performance of a traditional judicial function for which they are well qualified. Courts are comfortable interpreting and enforcing procedural requirements associated with trial-type hearings and determining when power has been properly delegated.

Another problem is that the due process tax idea does not tell us just how strictly the tax should be enforced. If eminent domain is overused to the point where uncompensated subjective losses and excessive use of government coercion become a problem, then the tax may be too low, and enforcement levels should increase. If eminent domain is confined to cases where these sorts of costs are minimal, then the tax may be about right (or conceivably may be too high). Whether eminent domain is being overused is an empirical question, as to which no good data exists. Nevertheless, there is at least some anecdotal evidence to suggest that eminent domain is being pressed into service in increasingly questionable ways. In addition to the controversial *Poletown* case, in which eminent domain was used to acquire a site for an auto assembly plant, recent decisions have involved the use of eminent domain to acquire land for retransfer to developers of casinos, race-tracks, and shopping centers.[323]

323. *See, e.g.,* Poletown Neighborhood Council v. City of Detroit, 304 N.W.2d 455 (Mich.1981); Southwestern Ill. Dev.

This may suggest the need for increased judicial vigilance in enforcing procedural rules associated with eminent domain.

What form might such increased vigilance take? One promising step, recently endorsed by a Pennsylvania court, would be to invalidate condemnations in which a public authority agrees to act as the agent for private developers, on the ground that this constitutes an impermissible subdelegation of the power of eminent domain without the consent of the legislature.[324] Another would be to give close scrutiny to statutes that confer "quick take" authority, whereby the condemnor can acquire title to land before legal issues associated with the authority to take and the amount of compensation have been resolved.[325] A third would be to insist on the right to trial by jury in takings cases.[326]

Auth. v. National City Env., L.L.C., 768 N.E.2d 1 (Ill. 2002) (invalidating use of eminent domain to acquire parking lot for auto race track); Casino Reinvestment Development Auth. v. Banin, 727 A.2d 102 (N.J. Super. Ct. Law Div. 1998) (invalidating use of eminent domain to acquire land and retransfer it to Donald Trump for development of a casino); Sun Co. v. City of Syracuse Indus. Dev. Agency, 625 N.Y.S.2d 371, 377 (N.Y.App. Div.1995) (upholding the use of eminent domain to construct a shopping center where it would "reduce urban physical and economic blight and promote economic revitalization of the acquisition site").

324. *In re* Condemnation of 110 Washington St., 767 A.2d 1154, 1159 (Pa. Commw. Ct. 2001) (holding that sovereign power of eminent domain "may not be delegated by agreement or contract").

325. *See, e.g.,* Joiner v. Dallas, 380 F.Supp. 754, 773 (N.D.Tex.), *aff'd*, 419 U.S. 1042 (1974) (suggesting that traditional due process requirements may be insufficient for quick taking proceedings); *see also* 6 PHILIP NICHOLS, NICHOLS' THE LAW OF EMINENT DOMAIN § 24.10[2][a] (Julius L. Sackman ed., 3d ed.

In any event, punctilious observance of the procedural and delegation requirements associated with eminent domain is probably the most promising available avenue for policing the choice between voluntary and coerced transactions. Certainly, it is more promising than demanding that courts engage in direct review of the efficiency of takings. And it provides a more targeted form of relief than would come about from increased judicial review of the "public use" requirement, which would require courts to adopt a restrictive understanding of the permissible ends of modern government, and contains a misplaced emphasis on ends rather than means—which is where the true problem lies.

1964) (discussing possibility of heightened due process scrutiny for quick takings).

326. There is no federal constitutional right to trial by jury in eminent domain proceedings. *See* United States v. Reynolds, 397 U.S. 14, 18 (1970). But juries are commonly used under federal and state condemnation statutes. *Id.* at 20; 1A NICHOLS, *supra* note 325, at § 4.104–105. Regulatory takings cases brought under 42 U.S.C. § 1983, in contrast, give rise to a right to jury trial. City of Monterey v. Del Monte Dunes at Monterey, Ltd., 526 U.S. 687, 722 (1999).

CHAPTER IX

EXACTIONS

So far, we have been concerned with cases in which the government condemns property or directly regulates it. By contrast, this chapter addresses situations in which the government (typically local, but sometimes state or even federal) permits a property owner to proceed with his or her proposed project, but subject to conditions that are generically referred to as exactions. An exaction, in contrast to a condemnation or direct regulation, takes the form of a *quid pro quo*. The government grants permission for development, but only if, in return, the owner agrees to donate certain property or money to the government. A distinct body of state and federal precedents assesses claims that these sorts of exactions constitute regulatory takings.

Exactions are extremely common.[327] Two principal contexts for the imposition of exactions are requests for zoning changes and for special use permits. Under traditional Euclidean zoning,[328] each parcel in a locality is zoned for certain speci-

[327]. For an overview, *see* ALAN A. ALTSHULER ET AL., REGULATION FOR REVENUE: THE POLITICAL ECONOMY OF LAND USE EXACTIONS (1993).

[328]. So named for Village of Euclid v. Ambler Realty Co., 272 U.S. 365 (1926), the case in which the Supreme Court upheld the constitutionality of comprehensive local zoning ordinances.

fied uses as part of a comprehensive or master plan.
In localities that still formally adhere to such zoning, code requirements for new construction are
often very restrictive, and landowners may find that
an economically viable development plan for a certain parcel requires an amendment to the zoning
code. Zoning authorities may impose exactions as a
condition of agreeing to the requested amendments.
Other jurisdictions have disavowed Euclidean zoning in favor of more flexible regimes. Under the
special use permit regime, for example, all major
development requires a special use permit from
zoning regulators. Regulators issue such permits
based on guidelines for the overall mix of uses the
community wishes to achieve, rather than a specific
zoning map for each parcel. Again, regulators may
impose exactions as a condition for issuing the
required special use permit.

Exactions can take several different forms, including required on-site land dedications, off-site
land dedications, or money payments. In some jurisdictions, exactions are set pursuant to statutory or
other formulas; in other jurisdictions, the exaction-
setting process is explicitly delegated to the discretion of individual regulators on a case-by-case basis.

When a landowner challenges an exaction as a
regulatory taking, the possible consequences differ
from challenges to direct regulation. When a court
finds that a direct regulation is a taking, the result
always favors developers of property: The government must either compensate the landowner for
restricting development or allow development to go

forward. By contrast, where a court holds that an exaction constitutes a taking, the effect on development is more uncertain. Of course, the government cannot impose the exaction, at least not without paying just compensation to the landowner. But the government can respond to the decision either by dropping the request for the exaction, or by denying permission to develop altogether. Thus, at least potentially, one result of a finding that an exaction is a taking is *less* development. Perhaps in part because challenges to exactions can backfire in this fashion, developers usually try to strike a deal with land use regulators, rather than litigating even those conditions they regard as excessive or inappropriate.[329]

There is a final important point about the relationship between challenges to direct regulations and exactions. Although the Supreme Court's two leading exactions decisions—*Nollan v. California Coastal Commission*[330] and *Dolan v. City of Tigard*[331]—clearly reflect the Court's recent shift toward affording greater protection to property rights, the doctrinal innovations of these decisions are confined to the special case of exactions and do not apply to challenges to direct regulation. In particular, the nexus and proportionality require-

329. *See* David A. Dana, *Land Use Regulation in an Age of Heightened Scrutiny*, 75 N.C. L. Rev. 1243, 1249 (1997) (arguing that developers avoid challenging conditions because they are "repeat players" in development and cannot afford to risk subsequent retaliation by land use regulators).

330. 483 U.S. 825 (1987).

331. 512 U.S. 374 (1994).

ments set forth in these decisions (discussed below) apply only to exactions. Thus, for example, there is no requirement that the burden of direct regulation must be roughly proportionate to the benefits produced by the regulation; indeed, the relationship between the benefits and burdens of regulation can be and often is highly disproportionate, without this resulting in a judgment that the regulation constitutes a taking. The special nexus and rough proportionality requirements for exactions are a product of the unconstitutional conditions doctrine, which serves as the underpinning of the decisions in *Nollan* and *Dolan* and has no application to direct regulations. The Supreme Court has confirmed this understanding.[332]

A. Exactions and the Unconstitutional Conditions Doctrine

The Court's special rules for exactions represent an application of the so-called unconstitutional conditions doctrine. This doctrine, in general form, says that the state may not condition the availability of

332. *See* City of Monterey v. Del Monte Dunes, 526 U.S. 687, 702–03 (1999) ("Although in a general sense concerns for proportionality animate the Takings Clause ... we have not extended the rough-proportionality test beyond the special context of exactions.... The rule applied in *Dolan* ... was not designed to address ... landowner's challenge[s] ... based not on excessive exactions but on denial of development.").

some discretionary benefit on an agreement by the recipient to waive or forgo a constitutional right.[333] For example, the government cannot offer employment to individuals conditioned upon their agreement never to engage in protected speech about public affairs.[334] Exactions fall within the general pattern of government conduct covered by the unconstitutional conditions doctrine: (1) A landowner/developer seeks a government benefit—amendment of the zoning code or issuance of a special use permit—that the government has broad discretion either to grant or deny. (2) The government conditions the receipt of this benefit on an agreement by the landowner/developer to transfer certain property to the government. (3) If the government were to appropriate the property directly from the landowner/developer, the Takings Clause would require the payment of just compensation. Thus, these exactions represent an attempt to condition the receipt of a discretionary government benefit on a waiver of a constitutional right, in this case, the right to just compensation for takings of property.

Although it is often stated as a universal truth, in practice, the unconstitutional conditions idea has been applied very unevenly. In some areas of consti-

333. *See* Dana, *supra* note 329, at 1245. For good general treatments of the unconstitutional conditions doctrine, and the analytic problems associated with it, *see* Frederick Schauer, *Too Hard: Unconstitutional Conditions and the Chimera of Constitutional Consistency,* 72 Denver L. Rev. 989 (1995); Kathleen M. Sullivan, *Unconstitutional Conditions,* 102 Harv. L. Rev. 1413 (1989).

334. *See* United States v. National Treasury Employees Union, 513 U.S. 454 (1995).

tutional law, such as rights of free speech and free exercise of religion, the prohibition of waivers of rights has been enforced quite strictly.[335] But in other areas, such as conditions on the exercise of protected reproductive choices, the Court has been much more reluctant to enforce the doctrine.[336] In still other areas, such as plea bargaining, where the prosecution agrees to a lesser charge or to recommend a more lenient sentence in return for the defendant's waiver of the constitutional right to a public trial, the doctrine has been ignored altogether.[337]

Given the uneven enforcement of the unconstitutional conditions doctrine, the initial question is whether exactions represent the type of constitutional condition as to which strict judicial supervision is appropriate. The Court's decisions in *Nollan* and *Dolan* are not much help in this regard. The Court in *Dolan* said: "We see no reason why the Takings Clause of the Fifth Amendment, as much a part of the Bill of Rights as the First Amendment or Fourth Amendment, should be relegated to the status of a poor relation in these comparable circumstances."[338] This implies that all constitutional rights should receive the same degree of protection under the unconstitutional conditions doctrine, and

335. *See, e.g.*, Perry v. Sindermann, 408 U.S. 593 (1972)Sherbert v. Verner, 374 U.S. 398 (1963).

336. *See* Webster v. Reproductive Health Servs., 492 U.S. 490 (1989); Harris v. McRae, 448 U.S. 297 (1980); Maher v. Roe, 432 U.S. 464 (1977).

337. *See, e.g.*, United States v. Mezzanatto, 513 U.S. 196, 209–10 (1995) (ruling that not even "gross disparity" in bargaining power will invalidate a plea agreement).

338. *Dolan*, 512 U.S. at 392.

extending close judicial scrutiny to exactions is simply a matter of bringing the Takings Clause into line with all other rights, like the First and Fourth Amendments. But, in fact, different rights receive vastly different degrees of protection under the unconstitutional conditions doctrine. So to say that the Takings Clause should not be relegated to the status of a "poor relation" for these purposes largely begs the question of what level of protection is appropriate and why.

When we try to dig deeper, at first it seems as if the Takings Clause is an implausible candidate for a significant degree of protection under the unconstitutional conditions doctrine. The right in question is not one as to which the idea of exchanging or selling rights seems repugnant, as would be the case with respect to the right to vote or the prohibition on slavery. Property rights are bought and sold all the time. Moreover, there does not seem here to be any pervasive problem of coercion or duress. Exactions reflect a straightforward consensual bargain: The government is in effect offering to sell development rights to the owner in return for the conveyance of property, and the owner has decided that the development rights are worth more than the property demanded in return. Finally, it is implausible to think that there are serious problems of unequal bargaining power or asymmetric information that render such deals generally suspect. Exactions are usually obtained from sophisticated real estate developers, who have as much, if not better, information about land values than does the government.

When we look harder, however, there may be some plausible arguments in support of a degree of judicial review of exactions. One possible argument is based on the fiscal illusion concern considered in Chapter IIIB2. An exaction allows the government to obtain property, not by condemning it and paying fair market value, but by granting certain development rights to the owner. The owner who agrees to this deal presumably values the development rights more than the value of the property given up. But the government may put a small value on the foregone development rights, in part perhaps because this value is hard to monetize. If this happens, then the government may suffer from the illusion that property it acquires through exactions is "free" or at least relatively cheap, and it may not have the same incentive to put this property to efficient uses that it would have if it had to pay fair market value for the property through condemnation.[339]

Another possible argument is based on process failure, considered briefly in Chapter IIIB3. The traditional sources of funding for local public goods like schools and parks are property taxes, sales taxes, and income taxes. But any attempt to tap these sources for additional revenue is likely to face stiff political resistance (in the case of property taxes) and/or result in taxpayers voting with their

339. *See* Thomas W. Merrill, Dolan v. City of Tigard: *Constitutional Rights as Public Goods*, 72 DENVER L. REV. 859 (1995).

feet by leaving for other jurisdictions (in the case of sales and income taxes). Exactions can be seen as an attempt to finance local public goods from another source: impositions imposed on the development of undeveloped land. Owners of undeveloped land may constitute a political minority with less clout than owners of developed land, and undeveloped land is not a movable asset, so there is no plausible threat of exit.[340] Thus, exactions may represent an effort to shift a disproportionate share of the burden of local taxation to a minority that cannot adequately protect itself in the political process. Certainly, together with the fiscal illusion argument, the possibility of process failure suggests that there is some justification for giving a degree of judicial scrutiny to exactions under the unconstitutional conditions doctrine.

B. *Nollan* and the Nexus Test

Prior to the 1987 decision in *Nollan v. California Coastal Commission*,[341] federal courts had been silent on the question of a federal constitutional standard for exactions. Many state courts, however,

---

340. For a debate over whether the threat of exit will protect developers from unduly burdensome exactions, *compare* Vicki Been, *"Exit" as a Constraint on Land Use Exactions: Rethinking the Unconstitutional Conditions Doctrine*, 91 COLUM. L. REV. 473 (1991) *with* Stewart E. Sterk, *Competition Among Municipalities as a Constraint on Land Use Exactions*, 45 VAND. L. REV. 831 (1992).

341. 483 U.S. 825 (1987).

had propounded constitutional tests for exactions as a matter of state constitutional law. All of these were means-ends tests, where exactions were conceived of as a means to offset or mitigate some of the harms or costs (*e.g.*, congestion, need for new roads) associated with new development. The tests differed in the kind or extent of connection they demanded between means and ends. Courts in a few States had held that exactions may be imposed under state constitutional principles only when they respond to community problems that are "specifically and uniquely" attributable to the development in question.[342] Most jurisdictions, however, opted for either a "reasonable relationship" test or a "rational nexus" test, both of which, in practice, required nothing more than some sort of cognizable relationship between the exaction and adverse community impacts that development may create.[343]

Nollan builds on these state precedents in that it also employs a means-ends test regarding the fit between the development conditions and the harm the development is expected to create. *Nollan*, however, propounds its "nexus" test under federal constitutional law and, at least arguably, the federal test is stricter than those previously employed by most state courts.

342. *See, e.g.*, Pioneer Trust and Sav. Bank v. Village of Mount Prospect, 176 N.E.2d 799, 802 (Ill.1961).

343. *See* John J. Delaney et al., *The Needs–Nexus Analysis: A Unified Test for Validating Subdivision Exactions, User Impact Fees and Linkage*, 50 Law & Contemp. Probs. 139, 146–56 (1987) (reviewing case law in various states).

The case itself involved a land dedication exaction. The Nollans owned a beachfront lot in Ventura, California, on which sat a dilapidated bungalow that the Nollans wanted to demolish and replace with a larger house. Under California law, the redevelopment project required a permit from the California Coastal Commission. The Commission granted the permit subject to the condition that the Nollans grant an easement allowing the public lateral access across the private portion of the beach behind their house. In reversing the state court holding that the easement condition was constitutional, Justice Scalia's opinion for the majority conceptualized the easement condition as presenting a classic unconstitutional conditions question: whether the State should be forbidden from achieving indirectly what it is forbidden from achieving directly (*i.e.*, transferring an easement to the public without the payment of compensation) or, alternatively, whether the State's greater power to deny a discretionary government benefit (*i.e.*, development permission for a new house) implies its power to place conditions on the grant of that benefit.

The majority opinion assumed that the Commission's stated purposes in imposing the easement condition—redressing the psychological barriers to public beach access that might result from new beachfront construction of the sort the Nollans proposed and preventing congestion on public beaches—were legitimate governmental ends. In the Court's view, however, there was an inadequate nexus—indeed, there was no nexus—between those ends and the means specified to serve them.[344] The Court held that the Coastal Commission had failed to meet the requirement that an "essential nexus" exist between "the condition" and the "justification for the prohibition" which would apply in the absence of satisfaction of the condition.[345]

One unresolved question regarding the *Nollan* nexus test is how far it departs from the deferential means-end review previously employed by the state courts in exaction cases and by the federal courts in reviewing exercises of the police power in general. In dissent, Justice Brennan maintained that the majority's nexus test "demands a degree of exactitude that is inconsistent with our standard for reviewing the rationality of a State's exercise of its police power for the welfare of its citizens."[346] Justice Scalia's majority opinion seemed to concede that as much:

We do not share Justice Brennan's confidence that the Commission 'should have little difficulty in the future in utilizing its expertise to demonstrate a specific connection between provisions for access and burdens on access' . . . that will avoid the effect of today's decision. We view the Fifth Amendment's Property Clause to be more than a pleading requirement, and compliance with it to be more than an exercise in cleverness and imagination. As indicated earlier, our cases describe the condition for abridgment of property rights

344. 483 U.S. at 838.

345. *Id.* at 837.

346. *Id.* at 842–43 (dissenting opinion).

through the police power as a '*substantial* ad-vanc[ing]' of a legitimate state interest.[347]

The *Nollan* majority, however, did not elaborate on the content of the emphasized adjective "*substantial*." The *Dolan* decision, discussed below, also suggests—although it does not directly confirm—that review of development conditions entails a closer degree of judicial scrutiny than rational basis review.[348] Exactly how much stricter remains uncertain.

C. *Dolan* and the Rough Proportionality Test

Seven years after *Nollan*, the Supreme Court established a second test for development conditions, which has come to be known as the "rough proportionality" test. The Court in *Dolan* made clear that rough proportionality is an additional requirement to *Nollan*'s nexus test. Thus, to be constitutional, a development condition must have a nexus to the anticipated harms resulting from the development *and* be roughly proportional. The key question about the *Dolan* test, unanswered by the opinion itself, is: roughly proportional to what?

347. *Id.* at 841.

348. 512 U.S. at 391 (adopting "rough proportionality" rather than "reasonable relationship" because the latter expression "seems confusingly similar to the term 'rational basis' which describes the minimal level of scrutiny under the Equal Protection Clause of the Fourteenth Amendment").

Dolan, like *Nollan*, involved a land dedication exaction. Florence Dolan owned a plumbing and electrical supply store in Tigard, Oregon, and applied for a permit to expand the store and pave over the parking lot. The permit was granted with the condition that she cede to the city a strip of land along a creek running through the property, to be used as a flood plain and the site for a public bicycle path. The majority in *Dolan* acknowledged that there was a nexus between both uses of the exaction and anticipated harms associated with the redeveloped store and new parking lot: The paving over of a larger percentage of Dolan's land would exacerbate flooding of the creek, and the vehicles that would be drawn to the enlarged store and parking lot would increase congestion in the downtown area. The Court found the exaction constitutionally impermissible, however, because the city had failed to quantify how much flooding would be prevented by the flood plain or how many car trips otherwise attributable to the new development would be avoided by the dedication of the bike path.

In determining what must be roughly proportional to what, it is useful to distinguish between three values: (1) the additional social costs attributable to the proposed development; (2) the fair market value of the property acquired by the exaction; and (3) the reduction in social costs attributable to the exaction. *Dolan* contains statements suggesting that the relevant comparison is between (1) and (3), that is, that the reduction in social costs from the exaction must be roughly proportionate to the social costs attributable to the development.[349] On at least one other occasion, the Court has suggested that the comparison is between (1) and (2).[350] Contrary to both these suggestions—at least if one adopts the fiscal illusion perspective on takings, according to which the objective of the compensation requirement is to assure that the government makes efficient use of acquired resources—the appropriate comparison should be between (2) and (3). In other words, the objective should be to assure that the use the government makes of the property—the reduction in social costs—is roughly proportionate to the fair market value of the property acquired; otherwise, the government is making an inefficient use of resources.[351] Given the opaqueness of the *Dolan* decision, it is perhaps not surprising that lower federal and state court precedents do not articulate

349. *See id.* at 394–95 ("the findings upon which the city relies do not show the required reasonable relationship between the floodplain easement and the petitioner's proposed new building"); *id.* at 395 ("the city has not met its burden of demonstrating that the additional number of vehicle and bicycle trips generated by petitioner's development reasonably relate to the city's requirement for a dedication of the pedestrian/bicycle pathway easement").

350. *Del Monte Dunes*, 526 U.S. at 702 (describing the *Dolan* test as addressing the proportionality of "conditions of development ... to the development's anticipated impacts."). Some state courts have adopted this reading of *Dolan*. *See, e.g.*, Ehrlich v. City of Culver City, 911 P.2d 429, 439 (Cal.1996) (stating that *Dolan* test asks whether the exaction "is more or less proportional, in both nature and scope, to the public impact of the proposed development").

351. *See* Merrill, *supra* note 339, at 885–86.

a clear, single interpretation of the rough proportionality test.

D. What Kinds of Exactions Are Subject to the Nexus and Rough Proportionality Tests?

Exactions can take a variety of forms, including on-site and off-site land dedications and agreements to pay cash. *Nollan* and *Dolan* leave unresolved whether the nexus and rough proportionality requirements apply to exactions other than land dedications, although they contain language suggesting they are limited to this type of exaction.[352] Some courts, however, have adopted the position that the nexus and rough proportionality tests apply to all development conditions, including purely monetary ones.[353]

We believe that *Nollan* and *Dolan* should be limited to exactions of land. This follows from the unconstitutional conditions doctrine that underlies the decisions, and, in particular, the requirement that the *quid pro quo* demanded by the government be a waiver of a constitutional right. Government appropriations of land without compensation violate

352. *See* Dana, *supra* note 329, at 1259–60.

353. *Id.* There is some evidence that, in the wake of *Nollan* and *Dolan*, land regulators have increased their reliance on monetary conditions as opposed to land dedications because they perceive the former to be more legally defensible. *See* Ann E. Carlson et al., *Takings on the Ground: How the Supreme Court's Takings Jurisprudence Affects Local Land Use Decisions*, 35 U.C. DAVIS L. REV. 103, 137–38 (2001).

the Takings Clause; government appropriations of cash ordinarily do not. Cash exactions are ordinarily not a taking because they can be rationalized as a form of taxation, and the Takings Clause constrains only the power of eminent domain, not the power of taxation. If this explanation is regarded as too formalistic, then, as an alternative explanation, cash exactions are not a taking because a general liability to make a cash payment to the government does not implicate any "private property," since the liability to pay in cash does not affect a discrete asset.[354]

Another, related question is whether the nexus and rough proportionality tests apply only to individually tailored, case-by-case conditions, as opposed to conditions set by a general formula or pursuant to a general practice. Courts in a number of States have read the *Nollan* and *Dolan* as limited to cases of individual tailoring.[355] While it is true that the courts at both the federal and state level have long been suspicious of case-by-case exercises of discretion in land use matters, we believe *Nollan* and *Dolan* cannot be read as limited to discretionary, case-by-case conditions. The unconstitutional conditions that provide the foundation for the

354. *See* Eastern Enter. v. Apfel, 524 U.S. 498, 539–47 (1998) (Kennedy, J., concurring); *id.* at 554 (Breyer, J., dissenting), discussed *supra* Chapter IV.

355. *See, e.g.,* Ehrlich v. City of Culver City, 911 P.2d 429, 433 (Cal.1996); Home Builders Ass'n of Dayton v. City of Beavercreek, 729 N.E.2d 349, 356 (Ohio 2000); Arcadia Dev. Corp. v. City of Bloomington, 552 N.W.2d 281, 286 (Minn.App.1996); Krupp v. Breckenridge Sanitation Dist., 19 P.3d 687, 696–97 (Colo.2001).

Court's doctrine do not distinguish between waivers of constitutional rules imposed by rule and those imposed by individual decisionmakers. And in fact, the exactions at issue in both *Nollan* and *Dolan* were imposed pursuant to, and consistent with, a general government practice.[356]

356. *See Nollan*, 483 U.S. at 829 (noting that 43 out of 60 coastal development permits had been conditioned by similar exactions); *Dolan*, 512 U.S. at 377–78 (noting that the exactions imposed by the city were consistent with a comprehensive plan adopted as part of the Community Development Code). The Court denied certiorari in a case that would have resolved the question whether the rough proportionality requirement applies to general requirements as opposed to case-by-case exercises of discretion. *See* Parking Ass'n v. City of Atlanta, 515 U.S. 1116 (1995) (mem.).

CHAPTER X

TAKINGS OF INTANGIBLE RIGHTS

The Takings Clause has traditionally been applied almost entirely to real property—land, buildings, and associated fixtures. Although land and buildings obviously continue to be important to both the economy and individual households, the centrality of these assets is diminishing relative to intangible property, such as intellectual property and regulatory rights (*e.g.*, broadcast licenses, professional licenses). For this reason, the application of the Takings Clause to intangible rights will probably become an increasingly important issue in the coming decades. A related issue is whether judicial, as opposed to legislative/regulatory, changes in the law can trigger takings liability on the part of the government. In other words, are existing legal rules recognized by courts themselves a kind of intangible right protected by the Takings Clause? This chapter reviews these looming, as yet unresolved, issues in takings law.

A. Judicial Takings

Most of the decisions we have discussed involve some change in law by a legislature or regulatory agency acting pursuant to authorizing legislation. But, of course, some of the most dramatic changes in law originate in new court decisions—decisions reversing or modifying previous precedents interpreting the common law, statutes or constitutions. From the property owner's perspective, the effect of a judicial opinion reinterpreting old legislation may be no different than new legislation. For example, the Hawaii Supreme Court has reinterpreted state water law dramatically to re-allocate water rights.[357] The same re-allocation of property rights could have been achieved by new legislation. In either case, individuals are in the same position, in that they no longer have the same water rights they once enjoyed.

The same position that is, except perhaps with respect to the Takings Clause. Under the regulatory takings doctrine, changes in legislation or regulation can trigger takings liability, at least in some instances. However, the federal and state courts have generally adhered to the position that judicial decisions cannot be challenged as regulatory takings—that judicial takings, as such, do not exist.[358]

There are a number of explanations for refusing to recognize judicial takings. For one thing, courts,

357. In fact, the Hawaii Supreme Court's reallocation of water rights is the exception that proves the rule: the reallocation was so extreme that, in a very unusual decision, the Ninth Circuit deemed the reallocation unconstitutional. *See* Robinson v. Ariyoshi, 753 F.2d 1468 (9th Cir.1985), *vacated on other grounds*, 477 U.S. 902 (1986).

358. *See generally* Barton H. Thompson, Jr., *Judicial Takings*, 76 Va. L. Rev. 1449, 1463–72 (1990).

unlike legislatures and many executive agencies, do not have the power to take property by eminent domain. Consequently, the basic logic for the regulatory takings doctrine recognized in *Pennsylvania Coal v. Mahon*[359] does not apply to courts: It is difficult to say that a court, by changing the law, is seeking to evade any obligation that *it* has to use the power of eminent domain, rather than the police power, to take property. For the same reason, it might be difficult to say where the property owner is going to get the just compensation due because of a judicial taking; if courts are not authorized to take property, then there may be no appropriated fund of money to pay judgments for judicial takings. Finally, and more cynically, courts will be reluctant to characterize their own actions a taking of property, since this would open them to public criticism and hamper their ability to resolve controversies as they see fit. For all these reasons, the courts have indulged in the fiction that, when they re-interpret property law, they never deny anyone a property right. Rather, they simply "clarify" that, although some members of society may have imagined that they had property rights, such rights in fact never existed.

The federal courts—in particular the Supreme Court—may be more willing to characterize state court action as a taking. Such a ruling would entail no self-criticism or limitation on federal court discretion and authority. And the Court has already held that the Takings Clause overrides any barrier

359.   260 U.S. 393 (1922).

to compensation grounded in state rules of sovereign immunity.[360] It would be but a small step to say that a federal court conclusion that a state court has committed a taking is just another federal judgment that the state legislature is obligated to pay on pain of contempt. In fact, in 1994, two Justices indicated a willingness to review a state court decision reallocating property rights as a possible violation of the Takings Clause. Dissenting from a denial of certiorari, Justice Scalia, in an opinion joined by Justice O'Connor, endorsed the petitioner's claim that the Oregon Supreme Court's reading of customary rights as guaranteeing public access to the dry sand portion of oceanfront beaches in that State "raise[d] a serious Fifth Amendment takings issue.... The issue is serious in the sense that it involves a holding of questionable constitutionality; and it is serious in the sense that the landgrab (if there is one) may run the entire length of the Oregon coast."[361] Justice Scalia stated that "[n]o more by judicial decree than by legislative fiat may a State transform private property into public property without compensation."[362] So it is at least possible that the Supreme Court will reconsider the conventional wisdom that judicial reinterpretation of the law cannot constitute a taking.

360. First English Evangelical Lutheran Church v. County of Los Angeles, 482 U.S. 304, 316 n.9 (1987).

361. Stevens v. City of Cannon Beach, 510 U.S. 1207 (1994) (Scalia, J., dissenting).

362. *Id.* (citing Webb's Fabulous Pharmacies, Inc. v. Beckwith, 449 U.S. 155, 164 (1980), and Lucas v. South Carolina Coastal Council, 505 U.S. 1003, 1031 (1992)).

The starting point in considering any judicial takings claim is to pay careful attention to the requirement that state has taken "private property" without just compensation. It is undoubtedly correct that "[a] person has no property, no vested interest, in any rule of the common law."[363] This is not because legal rules are intangible. It is because a rule of law lacks the defining characteristics of private property outlined in Chapter IV: it is not a discrete asset from which particular individuals have the right to exclude others.[364] Thus, no takings claim can be made for depriving an individual of a particular rule of law.

This does not mean, however, that particular legal rules do not create private property in other resources, tangible and intangible, in the sense that the rules authorize certain individuals to exclude others from discrete assets. When judicial decisions adopt legal rules that individuals rely upon to create private property rights in this sense, and then other judicial decisions change the law, such that these rights disappear or are severely qualified, the second decision can give rise to a takings claim.[365]

363. Munn v. Illinois, 94 U.S. 113, 134 (1877).

364. *Cf.* Thompson, *supra* note 358 at 1522–41. Thompson finds the "private property" issue more difficult in judicial takings cases. But he was writing at a time when the Court appeared to endorse a pure positivism approach to the meaning of property, and had not yet begun to develop a federal patterning definition. *See supra* Chapter IVA.

365. The Supreme Court in fact appeared to recognize this in its decision in *Munn*, 94 U.S. 113. After stating that "[a] person has no property, no vested interest, in any rule of the common law," the Court observed that nevertheless "[r]ights of property

For example, suppose state common law recognizes that a riparian owner has the right to exclude others from the portion of the sandy beach above the mean high water line. Then a subsequent state common law decision modifies this understanding and declares that a riparian owner has no right to exclude others from the sandy beach up to the vegetation line. The second decision has in effect abrogated the riparian owner's right to exclude from a discrete asset—the portion of the sandy beach between the mean high water line and the vegetation line—and would be vulnerable to a takings challenge. The claim is not that the former legal rule is itself private property, but that the former legal rule was used to establish private property and the new legal rule has taken this private property away.

B. Takings of Intellectual Property

The application of the Takings Clause to intellectual property—trademarks, copyrights and patents—has not yet been seriously tested in the courts. In a late Nineteenth Century case, the Supreme Court affirmed that the federal government is bound to honor the patents it issues.[366] Patents clearly qualify as private property—they entail the right to exclude others from particular inventions or processes, and they are commonly exchanged on

which have been created by the common law cannot be taken away without due process." *See* 94 U.S. at 134.

366. James v. Campbell, 104 U.S. 356 (1881).

a stand-alone basis. Patents have also long enjoyed the kind of specific and distinct guarantee of legal protection that gives rises to a reasonable invest-ment-backed expectation of continued legal recogni-tion.[367] At the same time, substantial popular and academic criticism has been directed at the breadth and strength of patent rights and the potential of those rights to compromise public interests. Consid-er the criticism directed at drug companies for maintaining high prices for patented AIDS-inhibit-ing drugs, and the consequent inability of AIDS victims in Africa to fully utilize such drugs. Or the concerns raised about the patenting of stem cell lines, which could be used to develop treatments for a range of diseases. Or, as discussed below, the criticism of the high prices charged for the patented antibiotic Cipro during the anthrax scare following the terrorist attacks of September 11, 2001. Some academic commentators have suggested that patent law should be re-interpreted to accommodate such public interest concerns.[368]

Would reducing patent rights—as through the introduction of a public interest exception to pat-

367. *See generally* Thomas Cotter, *Do Federal Uses of Intel-lectual Property Implicate the Fifth Amendment?*, 50 FLA. L. REV. 529 (1998) (providing a good review of relevant older prece-dents).

368. *See generally* Maureen A. O'Rourke, *Toward a Doctrine of Fair Use in Patent Law*, 100 COLUM. L. REV. 1177 (2000); David Lange, *Recognizing the Public Domain*, 44 LAW & CONTEMP. PROBS., AUTUMN 1981, at 147; Ian Ayres & Paul Klemperer, *Limiting Patentees' Market Power Without Reducing Innovation Incen-tives: The Perverse Benefits of Uncertainty and Injunctive Reme-dies*, 97 MICH. L. REV. 985 (1999).

ents, even a limited one for emergency situations—trigger takings liability for any resulting reduction in market value of those rights? For example, if a wonder drug for cancer were developed and patented, and the patent holder charged a price that generated extraordinary profits but threatened to bankrupt health insurers, could Congress impose a price cap on the patented drug? Or, if the patent holder refused to produce the drug at the capped price, could Congress grant a license to another manufacturer to produce the drug? Could the patent holder claim that the price cap and/or the compulsory license constitutes a regulatory taking requiring the payment of just compensation?[369] What if, to continue the theme of the last subsection, the courts construed the patent narrowly—more narrowly than previous precedents might have supported—to allow non-patent holders to market a closely related drug? Would this constitute a judicial taking?[370]

369. One could also imagine legislation that does not target particular patent holders but rather all patent holders or all patent holders in a certain industry. In fact, recent state proposals to cap prices of patented drugs apply quite broadly. *See, e.g., High Price of Prescription Drugs A Potent Issue in 2002*, THE BULLETIN'S FRONTRUNNER, April 1, 2002 (reporting that bills to deal with the costs of prescription drugs are under consideration in 37 state legislatures). As we discuss *supra* Chapter VIB5, the generality of regulation is a factor that weighs against finding a taking. Thus, from a Takings Clause perspective, patent reformers would be advised to pursue broad-based legislative measures. Broader measures, of course, may face greater political opposition than more narrowly focused measures.

370. The United States Patent and Trademark Office (PTO) awards patents for many processes and products that, upon the

Ruckelshaus v. Monsanto Co.[371] is the leading modern precedent on the question of whether, or when, the government is able to regulate the use of intellectual property to a substantial degree without running afoul of the Takings Clause. *Monsanto* concerned the submission to the Environmental Protection Agency (EPA) of data that Monsanto claimed qualified as trade secrets under applicable state law definitions. The Court affirmed that intangible property, such as trade secrets, can constitute private property under the Takings Clause. And it held that EPA's disclosure of trade secrets might well constitute a taking if it occurred during a period in which the law explicitly guaranteed

examination that attends patent infringement litigation, are found not to be properly patentable under current judicial formulations of patent law. It is also widely believed that the current judicial formulations of the scope of what is patentable and how broadly patents should be read has shifted in recent years in favor of patent holders. Consequently, there may be some "wiggle room" in patent law itself for the courts to hold, in response to a public health crisis, that the drug patents are invalid or not so expansive as to bar the lawful production, use and marketing of generic substitutes. Holdings of this sort would not constitute dramatic reversals of specific precedents—in most patent cases there are no specific precedents for the patent at issue—and would not be particularly vulnerable to "judicial takings" claims. Of course, the court primarily responsible for patent disputes— the United States Court of Appeals for the Federal Circuit— appears to be committed to a regime of strong patent protection and hence might not be open to such a narrowing interpretation. Another consideration is time: while Congress and the Executive can readily take quick action if the political pressures are sufficiently strong, the courts and the litigation process tend to move relatively slowly, particularly where, as in patent infringement litigation, intensive fact-finding is often required.

371.   467 U.S. 986 (1984).

protection from disclosure of information that the company had identified as trade secrets as part of its submission to EPA. In the absence of an explicit guarantee of protection from disclosure, however, the Court held that Monsanto had no reasonable investment-backed expectation because "[i]n an industry that long has been the focus of great public concern and significant government regulation, the possibility was substantial that the Federal Government . . . would find disclosure to be in the public interest."[372] *Monsanto* arguably suggests that the courts will read the scope of intellectual property rights narrowly in a takings challenge context where (as is true of the drug industry, for example) the affected property owners have long operated in a heavily regulated industry. But *Monsanto* does not answer the question of when, if ever, direct governmental modifications of unambiguous intellectual property rights are constitutionally permissible without compensation.

The recent controversy regarding Cipro provides a good vehicle for exploring the issues left open by *Monsanto*. Cipro is currently the antibiotic of choice for the treatment of anthrax, a naturally occurring bacteria that touched off a national panic after samples were sent through the mails in the Fall of 2001. Bayer, Inc. holds the patent on Cipro, and stood to earn massive profits because of the surge in demand caused by the anthrax scare. In response, the federal government threatened to compromise Bayer's patent rights by, among other things, pur-

372. *Id.* at 1007.

chasing generic substitutes for Cipro at much lower costs without compensating Bayer for patent infringement. Bayer responded to these threats by "agreeing" to provide the government with Cipro at a fraction of the then-prevailing market price.

Suppose the government had not reached an accommodation with Bayer, and Congress instead had passed legislation explicitly rendering Cipro's patent unenforceable vi-a-vis the government or competitor drug producers, without any obligation to provide compensation?[373] Or, suppose Congress legislated a price cap for anthrax-related antibiotics, thereby limiting the patent price advantage Bayer could command for Cipro? Would these actions con-

373. Federal law requires the United States to pay "reasonable and entire compensation" to a patent holder whenever "an invention described in and covered by a patent of the United States is used or manufactured by or for the United States without license of the owner thereof or lawful right to use or manufacture the same." 28 U.S.C. § 1498. Section 1498 has been read as a partial statutory expression or incorporation of the United States' compensation obligations under the Takings Clause, *see, e.g.*, Dow Chem. Co. v. United States, 36 Fed. Cl. 15 (1996); Gargoyles, Inc. v. United States, 37 Fed. Cl. 95 (1997), and it is not clear that Section 1498 imposes liability in any set of cases where the Takings Clause would not impose liability. Section 1498, however, is not properly regarded as coextensive with the Takings Clause because it excludes government actions that do not entail use of patented goods or services by or for the United States, but that may so devalue patent rights as to constitute takings, such as government price controls or government-ordered redistribution of patent rights to producers who do not or would not manufacture for government use. New legislation has recently been proposed that would dilute the compensation guarantee for patent holders. *See* The Affordable Prescription Drugs and Medical Inventions Act, H.R. 1708, 107th Cong., 1st. Sess. (2001).

stitute a regulatory taking under the Fifth Amendment, and if so, what compensation would be due?

These questions raise at least two puzzles under regulatory takings doctrine: (1) What is the scope of the property interest in an intellectual property right for purposes of applying either the categorical (total) or the *ad hoc* (partial) diminution in value tests? (2) Would such qualification of patent rights in response to a perceived public health crisis qualify for either the categorical exception from takings liability for nuisance regulation or the *ad hoc* factor that reduces the likelihood of takings liability when the government is regulating a noxious use? Since there are very few precedents other than *Monsanto* that have applied regulatory takings doctrine to intellectual property such as patents, all we can do is guess how, if at all, the courts will extrapolate from non-intellectual property precedents in addressing these doctrinal questions in the case of a patented drug such as Cipro. Let us consider each question in turn.

1. Defining the Scope of the Property

If the government were to transfer title in a patent to itself, or if it were to destroy an intellectual property right (as allegedly occurred with respect to the trade secret information in *Monsanto*), then there is no doubt this would constitute a taking. But when the government takes some action that results in devaluation of an intellectual property right, and this devaluation is alleged to constitute a regulatory taking, then the first thing we need to do is determine the scope of the relevant property, *i.e.*, the denominator, in order to determine the severity of the diminution in value. One can imagine a range of possible different definitions of the scope of the property held by a drug manufacturer such as Bayer with respect to a drug patent. Consider the following:

(a) The scope of the property in the patent could be defined by the right to exclude others from producing and marketing the drug or a close substitute described in the patent. Under this definition, price restrictions would not implicate the Takings Clause at all so long as the restrictions were not coupled with compulsory licensing to non-patent holders. This definition has the advantage that it tracks a common refrain in the federal common law of patent—that the essence of patent is the right to exclude.

Defining the scope of the patent property rights as the right to exclude does not mean that a system of compulsory licensing would constitute a *Lucas*-style wipeout triggering categorical review: It would have this effect only if the government completely abrogated the patentee's right to exclude. If the abrogation were only partial, then the patentee would still retain significant exclusionary power. For example, if the government in the Cipro crisis accorded only one other drug manufacturer (say Merck) a right to produce up to 50,000 tablets over the next year, Bayer would still retain some portion of its patent rights to exclude—that is, the right to exclude everyone except Merck and, even with respect to Merck, the right to exclude once the 50,000 tablets, one-year time limit has been met. Consequently, the government grant of a license to Merck presumably would be conceptualized as a partial diminution in value of a property right that falls within the scope of *Penn Central, ad hoc* review.

At least two possible objections to this analysis might be raised. First, one might conceive of each government-compelled license as a separate property interest in exclusion that the government has abrogated, such that the government's action in favoring Merck would constitute a complete taking of part of the property right. But, as discussed in Chapter IVB2, the right to exclude aspect of property is a generalized right to exclude an open-ended set of others. The government can abrogate a property owner's right to exclude in certain circumstances—for example where trespassers are acting under conditions of necessity—without defeating the conclusion that the owner has a property right. To treat the right to exclude as a bundle of exclusion rights, each one of which is itself a discrete property right, is to commit the fallacy of conceptual severance.

A second objection to the preceding analysis might build on an analogy to physical exclusion in the land context. When the government engages in a partial physical taking of land, for example by abrogating the right of a building owner to exclude the installation of a cable on the roof (as in *Loretto*), the courts categorically find a taking, even though the landowner retains the rights to exclude many other persons and entities. Why should the result be different in the context of patent law if the government were to allow Merck, but only Merck, to infringe Bayer's patent for 50,000 pills for one year? The answer is that property in land can and often is physically partitioned into smaller subdivisions, and it is well established that when the government takes by condemnation a partial interest in land, this is a taking. But the same conclusion does not follow when the government partially takes functional attributes of property, such as the right to alienate.[374] A regulation that eliminates the right to control the terms and conditions of a patent license with one company would seem to fall more naturally under the understanding that prevails with respect to partial abrogations of functional powers, such as the right to alienate, than under the understanding that prevails with respect to partial physical takings.

(b) The scope of the property in the patent could be defined in terms of the supernormal profits (monopoly rents) that would flow to the patent holder in the absence of government intervention, including ordinary patent monopoly rents that obtain under normal market conditions and extraordinary patent monopoly rents that obtain during an acute public health emergency. Under this definition, government regulation that nullified Bayer's ability to

374. *See* Andrus v. Allard, 444 U.S. 51, 67–68 (1979) (holding that abrogation of right to sell one type of personal property not a taking).

charge prices higher than those that would be obtained by the producer of a generic equivalent would qualify as a *Lucas*-type total wipeout. If, instead, the United States recognized Bayer's right to command a market price above what would be at the generic level, but regulated the price so as to limit Cipro's monopoly rents, or effectively reached the same result through a compulsory licensing regime, Bayer would suffer at most a partial diminution in value of its property interest, again, understood as the interest in receipt of full monopoly rents. In these circumstances, the *ad hoc* regulatory takings standard would apply.

(c) The scope of the property in the patent could be defined by the value of the extraordinary monopoly rents attributable to the unanticipated crisis or other event like the anthrax scare that gives rise to the perceived need for regulation. Under this definition, government regulation that eliminated the patent holder's extraordinary monopoly profits would constitute a total wipeout under *Lucas*. If, however, the patent holder retained some share of its extraordinary monopoly rents, for example, if government regulation was such that Bayer's patent-related profits during the anthrax scare only increased 30 percent instead of 300 percent (as they might in the absence of any government regulation), Bayer's claim would fall under the *ad hoc* takings test rather than *Lucas*.

(d) The scope of the property in the patent could be defined by the investment the patent holder has made in developing and marketing the patent. This

definition hearkens back to the public utility takings cases briefly discussed in Chapter VIC, where
the property is defined as the investment the utility
has made in plant and facilities designed to serve
the public, and a taking is said to occur when the
government fails to permit the utility to recover its
reasonable costs plus a fair, *i.e.*, risk-adjusted, return on investment. Under this conception of the
property, a patent holder would never suffer a total
wipeout under the *Lucas* rule even if it lost all
patent protection, since the patented product (here,
the drug Cipro) can always be sold at generic or
close-to-generic prices. Whether a taking would be
found under an *ad hoc* approach would presumably
turn on application of the unique *ad hoc* factors
used in public utility cases.

Definition (a) is problematic because (as explained above) it rarely, if ever, would trigger categorical review, and it does not in itself yield a useful
figure for purposes of *ad hoc* review. As explained in
Chapter VI, the diminution in value factor in *ad hoc*
review requires some numerical comparison of the
value of the property right before and after the
government action in question. In the context of the
right to exclude, it is very hard to envision how a
court could transfer into a fraction the percentage
loss of exclusionary rights without reference to one
or more of the financial impacts addressed in definitions (b), (c), and/or (d). Consider, for example, the
government's grant to Merck of a one-year right to
produce 50,000 Cipro tablets. How big a fractional
reduction in exclusionary property rights does that

government action represent? The only sensible way to answer that question would be to reframe the question in terms of the financial impact of the government action on the patent holder, as in how much of the total revenue that otherwise could be garnered by the patent monopoly does the government eliminate? Thus, even if courts nominally adhere to definition (a), they cannot stop there.

Definition (c) also seems problematic, given the definitional and empirical difficulties of distinguishing between ordinary and extraordinary monopoly profits. This definition also seems to countenance the "salami tactics" associated with conceptual severance, in that the power to earn monopoly rents is subdivided into two conceptually smaller sub-rights, making it easier to challenge price caps or compulsory licensing as either a categorical or *ad hoc* taking.

This leaves definitions (b) and (d) as the most likely candidates. The case for (b) would be that the very purpose of creating a system of patent rights is to allow patent holders to earn supernormal profits, *i.e.*, monopoly rents, for the term of the patent. Leaving the patent holder in a situation where it can only charge a normal competitive price for the drug is in effect to abolish the special rights associated with having a patent. A system of price caps or compulsory licensing that completely eliminated all monopoly rents would be the functional equivalent of abolishing the patent, and hence application of the categorical rule of *Lucas* would be appropriate in such circumstances. A system of regulation that eliminates some, but not all, monopoly rents, in contrast, would be appropriately addressed under the *ad hoc* takings standard.

Definition (d) might yield similar results if correctly implemented. In particular, if the regulator correctly calculated the risk premium required to set the rate of return for a highly speculative investment like a new drug, then just compensation should presumably include a significantly higher recovery than simply out-of-pocket costs plus a normal rate of return. But definition (d), with its implicit invocation of the public utility model, may be objectionable on conceptual grounds. The public utility model is designed to fix rates at a level that provides full and adequate compensation, but eliminates any supernormal profits due to the monopoly power that the utility enjoys. Patents and other intellectual property rights exist for the very purpose of conferring a monopoly that permits the patent holder to earn supernormal profits. Definition (d) and the public utility model also may entail high administrative costs relative to definition (b): a great deal of private industry data and expertise, for example, might be required to determine the appropriate risk premium to assign to the development of a drug. Administrative agencies might be able to develop sufficient capacity to gather and review the necessary data, but that too would be costly and courts would still need to struggle with the difficulties of meaningfully reviewing agency findings. So, on balance, we think that definition (b)—defining the scope of the property right as the ability to earn monopoly profits—is the best characterization of the scope of the property right for purposes of engaging in regulatory takings analysis.

2. *Public Policy Defenses*

Any attempt to regulate the prices charged for a patented drug in response to a perceived public health crisis might also benefit from what might be generically called public policy defenses. One such defense is the categorical rule recognized in *Lucas* that regulations that track the common law of nuisance are never deemed to be a regulatory taking. Another is the *ad hoc* factor recognized in *Pennsylvania Coal* and innumerable other cases that makes it more difficult to establish a taking when the government is regulating a "noxious use."

The *per se* exception for common law nuisance regulation almost certainly does not apply to an attempt to regulate high drug prices. Public nuisance law typically addresses a situation where some party is using his or her resources in a way that harms, by some spillover effect, the public; nuisance law is about action, harmful action, however defined. But the harmful aspect of the behavior of the patent holder (like Bayer with respect to Cipro) is not action but inaction—its inaction as regards the production and marketing of more pills at lower prices. We traditionally do not consider it a nuisance for someone to refuse to help the public, and that is essentially what the drug companies have been criticized for doing in the AIDS and Cipro/anthrax contexts.

The noxious use factor under *ad hoc* takings analysis, as we have discussed, should not be limited to the regulation of activity that would be a nuisance at common law.[375] Thus, the noxious use factor could more easily be interpreted to include industry behavior that directly or indirectly results in the public's need for lifesaving drugs not being satisfied or being satisfied with great distress and hardship. We suggested in Chapter VIB4 that the concept of noxious use should also probably be confined to harmful spillovers. But the case law is quite unformed in this regard, and under the discretionary *ad hoc* framework, courts could choose to— or choose not to—weigh the compelling public need for access to drugs at reasonable prices as an important factor in the multi-factor balancing analysis reserved for partial diminutions in value. The duration of the regulatory restrictions would also come into play, with less lengthy, time-constrained restrictions more likely to pass muster as constitutional measures even in the absence of compensation.

The AIDS and Cipro/anthrax cases suggest that the courts would have to struggle with other arguments from aggrieved patent holders in assessing any public interest justification for uncompensated modifications in property rights. First, the argument would be made that the "public interest" stops at U.S. borders and hence does not include

375. *See supra* Chapter VIB4.

foreign purchasers or potential purchasers of drugs. Second, a classic slippery slope argument would be advanced—that absent a constitutional check, uncompensated restrictions on the exercise of monopoly pricing power by the holders of drug patents could become commonplace, and substantial resources thus would be diverted from research and development of new useful processes and products.[376] Third, it would be argued that uncompensated modifications in patent rights may encourage greater investments by patent developers and holders in securing the election and continued support of "friendly" politicians, which also would translate into the diversion of resources away from research and development and might be regarded as weakening the integrity of the democratic process.

C. Breaches of Regulatory Contracts as Takings

Monsanto, as well as other older precedents, arguably suggest that regulated entities cannot expect the government to adhere to any particular future government policy affecting them in the absence of an express, explicit, written guarantee. However, two recent Supreme Court cases, *United States v.*

376. This argument was prominent in the financial press during the anthrax scare. *See, e.g.*, Lea Paterson, *US Patent Reappraisal Poses Long–Term Dangers*, THE TIMES (LONDON), Oct. 29, 2001 ("Any moves to dilute the Cipro patent would set a dangerous precedent, which could ultimately reduce the incentive for drug companies to carry out potentially life-saving research.").

Winstar Corp.[377] and *Mobil Oil Exploration and Producing Southeast, Inc. v. United States,*[378] suggest that "regulatory contracts"—implicit understandings in which the government agrees to adhere to a certain regulatory policy in return for some *quid pro quo* from the nongovernmental, regulated entity[379]—will be held to be legally enforceable in certain circumstances. By relaxing the standard for judicial recognition of a binding regulatory contract, the Supreme Court seems to be inviting litigation for contract damages and/or just compensation when the federal government alters its regulatory policy and hence devalues supposed property rights in alleged, albeit implicit, regulatory contracts. In that sense, the Court's shift on regulatory contracts mirrors its shifts in other takings areas, notably, the recognition of categories of categorical takings (Chapter V), application of unconstitutional conditions doctrine to exactions (Chapter IX), and relaxation of ripeness requirements (Chapter XI).

Winstar involved a suit by banks alleging that they had merged with other banks in reliance on an implicit promise by bank regulators that the institutions created by the mergers would not have to adhere to formally applicable loan loss reserve requirements. According to the banks, Congress breached this agreement and caused them financial

377. 518 U.S. 839 (1996).

378. 530 U.S. 604 (2000).

379. For a discussion of the complexities of determining exactly what the term "regulatory contract" means, *see* David Dana & Susan P. Koniak, *Bargaining in the Shadow of Democracy,* 148 U. PA. L. REV. 473, 480–85 (1999).

ruin when, in response to the burgeoning savings
and loan crisis, Congress passed legislation requiring strict, uniform adherence to loan loss reserve
requirements.[380] A majority of the Justices sided
with the banks, in effect abrogating older precedents that limited agencies' power to promise to
forbear from future regulation to situations where
(1) they act pursuant to clearly delegated legislative
authority, and (2) they make their commitments in
"unmistakable" language.[381]

Mobil Oil involved an alleged regulatory contract
between the United States and an oil company in
which the government purportedly agreed to freeze
regulations affecting offshore exploration in return
for payments from the company for exploration
rights. Although the written contract in question
nowhere stated that future oil exploration rights
were exempt from future environmental regulation—and indeed contained language to the contrary—the Court held that the subsequent adoption
of federal environmental legislation that delayed
exploratory drilling in the outer banks by requiring
an additional environmental analysis constituted a
contractual breach, requiring the payment of full
restitution.[382]

380. *See* Financial Institutions Reform, Recovery and Enforcement Act of 1989, *codified at* 12 U.S.C. §§ 1464 (t)(1)–(t)(3).

381. 518 U.S. at 860–91. For an analysis of the opinions in
Winstar, *see* Dana & Koniak, *supra* note 379, at 491–95.

382. 530 U.S. at 617–18. The sole dissenter, Justice Stevens,
also concluded that the United States had breached its contract
but argued that the remedy of full restitution was excessive
because North Carolina, not the United States, was primarily

As noted above in Chapter V, a number of formerly regulated monopolies have suggested that they have implicit regulatory contracts to the effect that they will be compensated for costs associated by the opening of the market to competition—by pro-competitive deregulation, in other words. The former monopolists style their claims as sounding in both contract and the Takings Clause.[383] The takings claim, as always, requires a careful analysis of whether the claimant has the requisite "private property." A legally recognized and enforced right to exclude competitors from a service territory might qualify as private property, but a mere expectation of continued monopoly status would not. Moreover, since deregulation generally does not produce physical invasions by the government or total economic wipeouts, any takings claim would have to be assessed under an *ad hoc* analysis, presumably the public utility standard.[384] As yet, however, the claim that deregulation constitutes a

responsible for Mobil's decision to abandon its exploration efforts in the Outer Banks. *See id.* at 636 (Stevens, J., dissenting).

383. *See* J. GREGORY SIDAK & DANIEL F. SPULBER, DEREGULATORY TAKINGS AND THE REGULATORY CONTRACT (1997).

384. Even if the right to exclude competitors constituted a legally cognizable property interest, partial or gradual deregulation might not be conceived of as a total taking of that property right. See the analogous discussion of patents, *supra*. Another

breach of contract and/or a compensable taking has not been tested in the courts.[385]

may be that, by and large, States have voluntarily (that is, without court order) compensated former monopolists for at least some of their so-called "stranded costs"—costs of infrastructure that is no longer profitable in light of deregulation. Perhaps the political clout of the former monopolists is too great for state officials to dare deny them compensation outright, *see* Daniel Farber, *Public Choice and Just Compensation*, 9 CONST. COMM. 279 (1992) (suggesting politically powerful interests normally will be compensated and hence will not need to resort to takings claims/litigation), or perhaps the former monopolists and the state officials are unsure what would happen in the courts and, averse to risk, they have decided instead to work out what is in effect a compromise solution on their own.

385. There are several possible reasons for this. One is that such claims are probably not ripe until deregulation schemes have been fully implemented, and full implementation has been delayed (in part by litigation over regulatory contract claims).

CHAPTER XI

LITIGATING TAKINGS CASES

Litigating takings cases presents a number of distinct challenges as a result of statutory and court-made procedural obstacles. As we have seen, in the last 15 years the Supreme Court has moved across a number of fronts to adopt substantive changes in takings law that favor aggrieved property owners. A parallel development has occurred in the federal procedural law of takings: Whereas once the Supreme Court bent over backwards to classify takings challenges as being too premature for adjudication or, failing that, limited adjudication to the state court system (where property owners in many States, such as California, faced notably unsympathetic judges), the Court has recently interpreted its takings procedure precedents in a manner that is more favorable to owners.[386]

This shift in the federal law of takings procedure could be just as important as a shift in the substantive takings law. Real estate development is a particularly time-sensitive industry, and procedural obstacles may be enough to dissuade property owners

386. The National Association of Home Builders has reportedly focused its recent lobbying efforts on procedural obstacles to litigating takings claims against States and localities in federal court.

from even trying to avail themselves of any substantive protection offered by the Takings Clause. This chapter explores the special procedural hurdles that apply to takings claims, whether they are brought against state and local governments or against the federal government.

A. The Relationship Between Substantive and Procedural Law

The special procedural obstacles that apply to takings claims flow from some of the unique attributes of the substantive law of takings. Takings claims, whether asserted in state or federal court, are subject to special "ripeness" requirements. These ripeness requirements, in turn, can be broken down into two subsidiary elements: a requirement that the government reach a "final" decision about the nature and scope of the challenged regulation, and a requirement that the property owner "exhaust" available remedies for obtaining compensation. Both the finality requirement and the exhaustion requirement grow out of unique aspects of takings law.

The most striking difference between the Takings Clause and other constitutional rights is that the Takings Clause does not prohibit government intrusions into a zone of autonomy, but rather requires the *payment of compensation* for government intrusions into a zone of autonomy. As the Supreme Court has observed:

> [The Takings Clause] does not prohibit the taking of private property, but instead places a condition on the exercise of that power. This basic understanding of the Amendment makes clear that it is designed not to limit the governmental interference with property rights *per se*, but rather to secure *compensation* in the event of otherwise proper interference amounting to a taking.[387]

Thus, in order to establish a takings violation, a property owner must show not only that private property has been taken by the government, but also that the government has refused to pay just compensation for it. The constitutional violation is not complete unless and until the owner shows *both* a taking *and* a denial of compensation.

The requirement that the property owner show a denial of compensation has important procedural implications, both for claims against state and local governments and against the federal government. Stated most broadly, it means that the property owner must ask for and be denied compensation before raising a takings claim. The "asking for" part will usually entail making some kind of claim or filing a specific kind of lawsuit, in other words, navigating additional procedural hurdles not pres-

---

387. First English Evangelical Lutheran Church v. Los Angeles County, 482 U.S. 304, 314–15 (1987). The Court's statement ignores the public use requirement, which, as we have seen *supra* in Chapter VIII, has been interpreted as prohibiting takings for private use, even with the payment of just compensation (although the Supreme Court has given great deference to legislatures in enforcing this limitation).

ent where other kinds of federal constitutional rights are at issue.

The other aspect of substantive takings law that affects procedures is limited to regulatory takings claims. As we discussed in Chapter VI, most regulatory takings claims are resolved under an *ad hoc* standard that is very sensitive to context. Even categorical claims based on complete loss of economic value will be highly dependent on the particular facts about the nature of the government regulation and the circumstances of the property. Determining what the landowner is permitted to do is complicated by the fact that land use regulation is a dynamic and, usually, multi-staged process. The government's first response to a proposal for development is usually not identical to its final response. The government will often change its mind about the proper regulatory limitations in reaction to objections from the owner, objections from neighbors who are affected by the proposal, and in light of new facts uncovered about the details of the project and its likely impacts.

All this means that "a landowner may not establish a taking before a land-use authority has the opportunity, using its own reasonable procedures, to decide and explain the reach of a challenged regulation."[388] In other words, landowners must endure procedural obstacles above and beyond those that confront other types of constitutional plaintiffs.

388. Palazzolo v. Rhode Island, 533 U.S. 606, 620 (2001).

These substantive features of takings law explain the two-part ripeness test that the Supreme Court has articulated for takings challenges. The first part of the test—the final land use determination—goes to the question whether the nature of the government regulation and its impact on the property owner is sufficiently fixed to allow a court to apply either the *Lucas* total wipeout test or the *ad hoc* takings standard.[389] The second part of the ripeness test—the exhaustion of available compensation remedies requirement—is grounded in the notion that a federal constitutional violation does not occur until just compensation has been denied. Thus, where procedures exist for claiming compensation, those procedures must be used before the courts will exercise jurisdiction over a takings action.[390]

B. The Finality Requirement

The finality requirement, on its face, sounds sensible enough: Until the exact parameters of permis-

389. *Williamson County* is typically cited as the case that first definitively expressed this requirement. *See* Williamson County Regional Planning Comm. v. Hamilton Bank of Johnson City, 473 U.S. 172, 186 (1985) ("a claim that the application of government regulations effects a taking of a property interest is not ripe until the government entity charged with implementing the regulations has reached a final decision regarding the application of the regulations to the property at issue").

390. Again, *Williamson County* is typically cited as the definitive case on this point. *See Williamson*, 473 U.S. at 195 ("if a State provides an adequate procedure for seeking just compensation, the property owner cannot claim a violation of the Just Compensation Clause until it has used the procedure and been denied just compensation").

sible land use development of a parcel are finally determined by the government, it is impossible for the trier of fact to determine whether, or to what extent, a regulation has reduced the value of some item of property. The ambiguity in the case law relates to how far the property owner must persist in challenging the parameters of permissible development. Is it enough for the owner to submit a development plan and receive a denial of permission? (Generally no; see below.) Must the owner seek a variance or other administrative relief from the generally applicable regulations that formed the basis of the denial of development permission? (Generally yes; see below.) If variances or other administrative relief are denied, must the owner seek approval for a second less extensive development plan, or a third, or a fourth? (Unclear; see below). In other words, at what point can the owner safely conclude that it is unreasonable and/or futile for her to make further efforts to secure modifications in the regulations and instead begin to pursue a takings claim in court?

The Court has not definitively answered the question of precisely when property owners may say "enough is enough" and head to court. A line of cases in the 1980s—*Hodel v. Virginia Surface Mining & Recreation Association*[391], *Williamson County Regional Planning Commission v. Hamilton Bank*

391. 452 U.S. 264 (1980).

of Johnson City,[392] and *MacDonald, Sommer & Frates v. Yolo County*[393]—suggest that the burden on the owner is substantial. In both *Williamson* and *MacDonald*, the owner submitted a development plan, received a denial of permission based on the inconsistency of the development plan with generally applicable requirements, and then failed formally to apply for administrative relief or variances. In holding that these owners' cases were unripe, the Court indicated that, at a minimum, a landowner must seek variances from generally applicable requirements before bringing a takings claim. The tenor and tone of the opinions, moreover, suggest that owners must do even more, although the Court conceded that the finality requirement should not be an excuse for strategic stonewalling on the part of local governments.[394]

Three more recent takings cases, while purporting to reaffirm *Williamson* and *MacDonald*, suggest a relaxation of the finality requirement. In *Lucas*,[395] the majority of Justices refused to consider the argument that the case was unripe because Lucas had not sought administrative relief from the development ban, even though a system for such relief was established after the development ban went into effect in response to landowner complaints. In

392.   473 U.S. 172 (1985).

393.   477 U.S. 340 (1986).

394.   *See MacDonald*, 477 U.S. at 350 n.7 ("A property owner is of course not required to resort to piecemeal litigation or otherwise unfair procedures....").

395.   Lucas v. South Carolina Coastal Council, 505 U.S. 1003, 1010–14 (1992).

Suitum v. Tahoe Regional Planning Agency,[396] the Court held that a challenge to a development moratorium was ripe even though the exact application and value of transferable development rights available to the landowner were uncertain to some extent. And in *Palazzolo v. Rhode Island*,[397] the Court held that there had been a final determination of the permissible development of a parcel containing wetlands and uplands even though the landowner had not sought *any* development permission specifically addressing the upland area.

The implicit thrust of these cases—and especially *Palazzolo*—is that the Court has come to view strict application of the final land use determination requirement as asking too much of landowners. Recent empirical literature regarding the disposition of takings cases by federal district courts, however, suggests that the lower federal courts continue to apply the ripeness requirements of *Williamson* and *MacDonald* with some vigor.[398]

396. 520 U.S. 725, 737 (1997).

397. 533 U.S. 606 (2001). As Justice Ginsburg pointed out in her dissent, "[a]s presented to the Rhode Island Supreme Court, Anthony Palazzolo's case was a close analogue to *MacDonald*." *Id.* at 646 (Ginsburg, J., dissenting).

398. *See* John J. Delaney et al., *Who Will Clean Up the Ripeness Mess? A Call for Reform So Takings Plaintiffs Can Enter the Federal Courthouse*, SF 64 ALI–ABA 57, 60 (May 3, 2001) (discussing results of a land use survey showing that "83 percent of takings cases with an opinion reported by a U.S. district court were dismissed on ripeness or abstention grounds. Of those property owners who could afford to bring an appeal, 64 percent still faced dismissal on jurisdictional grounds. On the average, the minority of property owners who received a determi-

C. Exhaustion of Remedies

As a general rule, plaintiffs who believe that they
have been deprived of some federal constitutional
right by state or local officials acting under color of
law may bring an action in federal district court
under 42 U.S.C. § 1983 without first bringing any
sort of state lawsuit, even when state court actions
addressing the underlying behavior are available.
For example, when an individual claims that his
Fourth Amendment rights have been violated by an
unwarranted search or seizure, he may bring a
Section 1983 action without first bringing a state
court tort action for trespass or battery. In other
words, Section 1983—the primary vehicle by which
citizens seek damages for federal constitutional
wrongs committed by state or local officials—has no
exhaustion requirement.[399]

Nonetheless, in the context of federal constitutional claims based on the Takings Clause, the
Supreme Court has held that property owners first
must seek compensation in state actions (typically,
state inverse condemnation actions) before seeking
federal court review, at least where state law affords adequate procedures for claiming compensation for the loss in value of the property at issue.

nation that their takings claim could be adjudicated on the
merits endured 9.6 years—almost a decade—of negotiation and
litigation.").

399. *See* Patsy v. Florida Bd. of Regents, 457 U.S. 496, 500–
16 (1982); *Williamson*, 473 U.S. at 192.

There are a few unusual cases where a federal district court can exercise original jurisdiction over a takings claim in the absence of any preceding state action, most notably where there are other claims with an independent, adequate basis for federal jurisdiction, and the district court exercises jurisdiction over the Section 1983 takings claim as a matter of pendent or supplemental jurisdiction.[400] In general, however, property owners must begin in the state courts.

It is not entirely clear whether the owner must specifically seek compensation based on the federal Takings Clause in state court in order to meet the Supreme Court's ripeness requirements; it may be adequate for the landowner to bring a state inverse condemnation action based on state law grounds for seeking compensation. In order to be sure that federal ripeness requirements have been met, however, a landowner is safest specifically alleging federal as well as state grounds, if any, in the state action. Note, however, that doing so almost guarantees that relitigation of the takings claim in federal court will be challenged—usually successfully—on claim preclusion grounds. Indeed, even where a litigant does not specifically plead the Takings Clause in the state court action, the state court action is bound to encompass many of the key issues under Takings Clause tests. As a result, there is almost no way to meet ripeness requirements for a takings challenge in federal court and to avoid

400. *See, e.g.,* City of Chicago v. International College of Surgeons, 522 U.S. 156 (1997).

issue preclusion in federal court regarding key issues implicated by the takings claim.

This gives rise to what has been called the *"Williamson* trap."[401] Filing a federal district court takings action after bringing a state inverse condemnation proceeding is nominally permissible under the ripeness rules, but is often rendered pointless (or something close to it) under preclusion rules. As a practical matter, therefore, property owners' only route to federal court review in a typical land use case involving state or local regulation is by means of a petition for certiorari to the Supreme Court from an adverse state supreme court judgment. Such petitions, of course, are only rarely granted.

The rule that property owners generally must start in state court means that, to a significant degree, federal takings law is a kind of co-venture between the Supreme Court and the various state supreme courts. Under the Supremacy Clause of the federal Constitution, of course, the Supreme Court has the last say. But the Supreme Court can, at most, hear only one or two land use cases each Term, so that, in most instances, the final word of the state supreme court in a land use case is the final word, period. The Supreme Court's ripeness rules are thus in keeping with its view, recently reaffirmed in *Solid Waste Agency of Northern Cook*

401. *See* Madeline J. Meacham, *The Williamson Trap*, 32 URBAN LAW. 239 (2000); *see also* Thomas E. Roberts, *Procedural Implications of Williamson County/First English in Regulatory Takings Litigation: Reservations, Removal, Diversity, Supplemental Jurisdiction. Rooker–Feldman and Res Judicata*, 31 ENVT. L. REP. 1353 (April 2000).

County v. United States Army Corps of Engineers,[402] that land use is a quintessentially local matter and that the federal government and federal law have, at most, a diminished role to play in this area. At the same time, the Court's ripeness rules stand in tension with the principle that federal constitutional guarantees, precisely because they are federal, should not turn on the particular state where a litigant lives or holds property.[403]

D. The Tucker Act

The discussion in the two previous subparts applies with full force to claims against state and local governments. Takings claims against the federal government are subject to the same finality requirements as claims against state and local governments. With respect to the exhaustion requirement, however, federal takings claimants obviously have no obligation to submit claims in state court before they turn to federal court. Nevertheless, federal takings claimants face a distinct but closely analogous kind of exhaustion barrier. Under the Tucker Act,[404] the United States district courts and the Court of Federal Claims in Washington, D.C. (court of claims), have concurrent jurisdiction over any

402. 531 U.S. 159, 172–73 (2001).

403. Of course, as discussed *supra* in Chapter IV, an essential question in federal takings law—what is property—does turn substantially on the particulars of the state law where the litigant claims a taking occurred.

404. 28 U.S.C. § 1346(a)(2)(1988).

claim against the United States under the Constitution (including takings claims) for amounts not exceeding $10,000. For claims exceeding $10,000, the Tucker Act vests exclusive jurisdiction in the court of claims.

The most significant legal doctrine that has emerged under this statutory scheme is that a federal district court exercising general federal question jurisdiction may not adjudicate a claim that the federal government has committed a taking as long as Congress has not foreclosed the claimant's remedy under the Tucker Act.[405] This "Tucker Act doctrine" is closely analogous to the exhaustion doctrine that applies to state and local takings claims— and it has the same source in the unique nature of the constitutional right created by the Takings Clause. Because the Clause creates a right of compensation, not injunctive relief, no constitutional violation occurs until it is clear that the federal government has denied just compensation. Moreover, the Court has held, the Clause "does not require that just compensation be paid in advance of or even contemporaneously with the taking. All that is required is the existence of a reasonable, certain and adequate provision for obtaining compensation at the time of the taking."[406] Thus, as long the Tucker Act remedy is available, it is premature to allege that the federal government has

405. *See, e.g.*, Preseault v. ICC, 494 U.S. 1, 11 (1990); Regional Rail Reorganization Act Cases, 419 U.S. 102, 124–25 (1974).

406. *Preseault*, 494 U.S. at 11 (citations and quotations omitted).

violated the Constitution. Of course, under general principles of preclusion, if the court of claims decides the challenged action is not a taking, the property owner will not be able to relitigate this issue in a federal district court of general jurisdiction. In practice, therefore, if the Tucker Act remedy is available, it is the court of claims or nothing.

By and large, lower federal courts have rejected litigants' efforts to avoid the Tucker Act doctrine by disaggregating their money claims and/or by styling their claims as claims for nonmonetary relief.[407] The Supreme Court has been less consistent. In a trend that parallels developments recounted above with respect to exhaustion of state remedies, the Court has shown an increased willingness of late to find that the Tucker Act remedy is "impractical" and hence unavailable.[408] Such a finding permits the Court to adjudicate takings claims that have been raised in the lower federal courts in cases founded on general federal question jurisdiction.

Ordinarily, the Supreme Court's inconsistent enforcement of the Tucker Act doctrine would be expected to give rise to widespread attempts to evade the rule that all takings claims above $10,000 must be channeled through the court of claims. But, in recent years, the court of claims and Federal Circuit have rendered some notable pro-property

407. *See* Section 2306, *Concurrent Jurisdiction With District Courts Under Tucker Act*, 32B AM. JUR. 2D FEDERAL COURTS (1996) (collecting and summarizing relevant case law).

408. *See, e.g.*, Eastern Enterp. v. Apfel, 524 U.S. 498, 519–22 (1998); Babbitt v. Youpee, 519 U.S. 234, 243–45 (1997); Hodel v. Irving, 481 U.S. 704, 716–18 (1987).

rights decisions under the Takings Clause.[409] Consequently, notwithstanding the fact that litigating in Washington, D.C. may be inconvenient for some property owners, and that there is no right to trial by jury in the court of claims,[410] as a general matter, property owners have been content to have takings claims against the federal government heard by the court of claims rather than the regional district courts.

E.   The Consequences of Procedural Delay

We close with two final twists concerning the consequences of procedural delay. One twist is the possibility that the procedural hurdles to mounting a takings claim associated with ripeness requirements might themselves give rise to delays that could be characterized as a taking. The other twist

409.   *See, e.g.,* Loveladies Harbor Inc. v. United States, 28 F.3d 1171 (Fed.Cir.1994) (upholding a total taking finding even though the developer was permitted to build upon a substantial area prior to the wetland permit denial at issue); Florida Rock Ind., Inc. v. United States, 45 Fed. Cl. 21 (1999) (finding a taking under *Penn Central* analysis in a wetland permit case after previously finding a total taking under *Lucas* and being reversed by the Federal Circuit).

410.   *See, e.g.,* KLK, Inc. v. United States Dep't of Interior, 35 F.3d 454, 458 (9th Cir.1994) (affirming that the "Tucker Act does not provide for jury trials" in inverse condemnation/takings cases). By contrast, in takings actions against state and local governments brought under Section 1983, litigants have Seventh Amendment rights to have issues of fact and mixed issues of fact and law submitted to a jury. *See* City of Monterey v. Del Monte Dunes, 526 U.S. 687, 709–11 (1999).

is that the Court's relaxation of ripeness requirements, if coupled with delays attributable to the
owner, could give rise to a government defense
against takings liability based on the statute of
limitations or laches.

As noted in Chapter VII, the Supreme Court in
*First English Evangelical Lutheran Church v. Los
Angeles County*[411] held that temporary takings of
property are subject to the just compensation requirement of the Takings Clause no less than permanent takings of property. Thus, for example, if
the government condemns property for a limited
period of time, such as the duration of a national
emergency, the limited duration of the government
action does not affect the question whether a taking
has occurred—only the question of how much compensation needs to be paid.

First English appears to articulate another type
of categorical rule: the Court held that temporary
actions that otherwise would be takings had they
been permanent always trigger a just compensation
duty. But like the categorical rule in *Lucas*, the
categorical rule in *First English* contains an exception: The Court in *First English* explained that its
rule regarding temporary takings does not apply to
"normal delays in obtaining building permits,
changes in zoning ordinances, variances, and the
like."[412]

411. 482 U.S. 304 (1987).

412. 482 U.S. at 321.

In *Tahoe–Sierra Preservation Council, Inc. v. Tahoe Regional Planning Agency*,[413] the Supreme Court endorsed a broad construction of the "normal delays" exception to categorical temporary takings liability, and recognized an exception for "temporary" growth moratoria as well—even one lasting 32 months. Indeed *Tahoe–Sierra*, which employs much the same rhetoric and argumentation as the dissent in *First English*, leaves open the question of what, if anything, remains of *First English*'s categorical rule that temporary actions that otherwise would be takings had they been permanent always trigger a just compensation duty.[414]

But *Tahoe–Sierra* establishes only that regulatory delay, as long as it can fairly be characterized as "temporary," does not trigger *per se* takings liability. The decision expressly reserves judgment on the question whether such a delay might be found to be a taking under an *ad hoc* analysis. Moreover, the decision explicitly excludes from its holding cases where regulators, instead of acting "diligently and in good faith," are simply "stalling."[415] Thus, the possibility remains that regulators may be deemed to have committed a compensable taking if they drag out the procedural prerequisites to establishing a takings claim too long.

413. 122 S.Ct. 1465 (2002).

414. The Court in *Tahoe–Sierra* did not purport to overturn *First English* in any respect, so future litigants are free to argue on the basis of both *First English* and *Sierra–Tahoe*, notwithstanding the tensions between the two opinions.

415. 122 S.Ct. at 1485.

On the other side of the coin, delays by the owner in bringing a development proposal to fruition can give rise to government defenses based on the statute of limitations or laches. Consider by way of illustration the facts of *Palazzolo*. Palazzolo was a shareholder in a corporation that acquired property in Rhode Island in 1959, which corporation unsuccessfully attempted in 1962 and 1966 to secure permits to fill the property and proceed with development. The corporation dissolved and Palazzolo acquired the land outright in 1978. In 1983 and 1985, Palazzolo made further efforts to secure permits for filling and development of the property. When these efforts were rebuffed, he brought an action for inverse condemnation in state court.

The Supreme Court held that Palazzolo's takings claim became ripe in 1985, when the last of his attempts to secure development permission was denied.[416] Presumably, this was also the time when his cause of action for a regulatory taking accrued—this was when the facts about the permissible scope of development became sufficiently final that it was possible to adjudicate either a *Lucas* total takings claim or an *ad hoc* takings claim. Thus, the statute of limitations for an action for inverse condemnation began to run in 1985.

Although *Palazzolo* did not present any question about the statute of limitations or laches, it is possible to imagine variations on the facts of the case that would. Suppose, for example, that the attempt by the corporation to secure permission to

416. *Palazzolo*, 533 U.S. at 617–26.

develop in 1966 gave rise to a ripe claim for a regulatory taking. This would mean that the statute of limitations started to run in 1966. The transfer of ownership from the corporation to Palazzolo should not interrupt the running of the statute, since Palazzolo succeeded to all rights of the corporation, including any cause of action for a regulatory taking.[417] Provided the state statute of limitations in Rhode Island is anything short of 20 years,[418] Palazzolo's claim would then have been barred by the statute of limitations. Or, if there is no clear statute of limitations for such claims, the passage of such a long period of time would mean almost certainly that it would be barred by laches.

The point is that to the extent the Court is relaxing the ripeness requirements for bringing regulatory takings claims—and *Lucas*, *Suitim* and *Palazzolo* suggest that it is—then this is something of a double-edged sword for property owners. It is true that this relaxation permits them to sue in court at an earlier point in the regulatory process than previously had been thought to be the case. But it also means that the statute of limitations on regulatory takings claims starts running at an earlier

417. In the law of adverse possession, for example, the transfer of property from one true owner to another does not restart the clock ticking for purposes of prosecuting an action in trespass against an adverse possessor. *See, e.g.,* Howard v. Kunto, 477 P.2d 210 (Wash.Ct.App.1970).

418. The state statute of limitations for takings claims are generally substantially less. For a discussion of state limitations and how they have been applied, *see generally* Charles C. Marvel, *State Statute of Limitations Applicable to Inverse Condemnation or Similar Proceedings*, 26 A.L.R. 4TH 68 (1983).

date. If property owners put off suing, perhaps because of an unwillingness to incur the risk and expense of litigation, then their constitutional claim for compensation will eventually expire. The government would then acquire what amounts to a prescriptive easement or servitude permitting continued regulation of the property—perhaps in ways that would have been deemed to be a taking if litigation had been prosecuted in a timely fashion.

CHAPTER XII

CONCLUSION

Takings law is often characterized as "chaotic," "muddled" or "incoherent."[419] Whether these characterizations are fair depends, to a large extent, on what one expects takings law to accomplish. If one expects this law to identify all circumstances when individuals who experience disproportionate losses because of government action should be compensated, then the law does indeed seem unsatisfactory. To take but one example, some owners who experience trivial losses—like Ms. Loretto who objected to the installation of a cable television wire on the roof her apartment[420]—are always entitled to compensa-

419. *See, e.g.*, BRUCE A. ACKERMAN, PRIVATE PROPERTY AND THE CONSTITUTION 8 (1977) (noting that takings law is generally regarded as "a chaos of confused argument"); John D. Echeverria, *Takings Law Symposium: Does A Regulation that Fails to Advance a Legitimate Governmental Interest Result in a Regulatory Taking?*, 29 ENVTL. L. 853 (1999) (describing regulatory takings law as "famously muddy"); Carol M. Rose, Mahon *Reconstructed: Why The Takings Issue is Still a Muddle*, 57 S. CAL. L. REV. 561 (1984) (attributing the takings "muddle" to continuing tensions within American political culture); Jeanne L. Schroeder, *Never Jam To-day: On the Impossibility of Takings Jurisprudence* 84 GEO. L.J. 1531, 1531 (1996) (describing takings law as "a top contender for the dubious title of 'most incoherent area of American law' ").

420. Loretto v. Teleprompter Manhattan CATV Corp., 458 U.S. 419 (1982), discussed *supra* Ch. V.

tion; other owners who experience very large loses—such as Mr. Hadacheck who had his brick yard in Los Angeles shut down[421]—get nothing. These sorts of results are difficult to justify in terms of any general theory of distributive justice or social efficiency.

But, if we bear in mind that the Takings Clause is at root a limitation on the power of eminent domain, much of the seeming incoherence melts away. The relevant question now becomes: Is the government engaged in the functional equivalent of a nonconsensual transfer of a resource that ordinarily would have to be purchased? The eminent domain perspective restores the "private property" language of the Clause to the picture, and helps us to understand that this refers to discrete assets subject to exclusion rights that are exchangeable on a stand-alone basis. It also helps us to understand how the Court's categorical and *ad hoc* rules function as decisional devices for sorting government actions into those that are the functional equivalent of eminent domain, and those that are properly regarded as exercises of the police power. Other parts of the picture, such as the fair market value measure of just compensation, the special rules for exactions, and the peculiar ripeness requirements for litigating takings claims, also start to make more sense.

421. Hadacheck v. Sebastian, 239 U.S. 394 (1915) (upholding law barring operation of brick mill in residential area as valid exercise of police power even though brick yard was built before the area turned residential and the regulation resulted in nearly complete loss of value).

None of this is to suggest that there are obvious answers to all, or even most, of the problems presented by the Takings Clause. Judges and commentators will no doubt continue to disagree about such things as how far to specify a federal definition of private property, the proper domain of categorical and *ad hoc* takings analysis, and whether the government should be permitted to condemn and retransfer property to private parties. But so long as we do not overload the Takings Clause with expectations it cannot fulfill, takings law is probably no more chaotic or muddled than is, say, the law of freedom of speech or equal protection. To be sure, it is no less difficult either. But to say that the law is difficult is not the same as to say it is beyond comprehension. We hope that we have shown that takings law is at least comprehensible.

TABLE OF CASES

References are to Pages.

277

*

INDEX

References are to pages.

283

LITIGATING TAKINGS CASES—Cont'd

MADISON, JAMES

MARINA

MINERAL RIGHTS

MINING

MONOPOLY RENTS

MONOPOLY SELLERS

References are to pages.